USEFUL MEASUREMENTS
FOR VIOLIN MAKERS

A Reference for Shop Use

by Henry A. Strobel

BOOK ONE OF THE STROBEL SERIES FOR VIOLIN MAKERS:

Book One	*Useful Measurements for Violin Makers*
Book Two	*Violin Maker's Notebook*
Book Three	*Health of the Violin, Viola, and Cello*
Book Four	*Art & Method of the Violin Maker*
Book Five	*Violin Making, Step by Step*
Book Six	*Cello Making, Step by Step*

Henry Strobel, Violin Maker & Publisher

10878 Mill Creek Road, Aumsville OR, 97325 USA

For more information visit our World Wide Web Address:
http://ourworld.compuserve.com/homepages/Henry_Strobel

Library of Congress Catalog Card Number:
89-90382

ISBN 0-9620673-2-6

Sixth Printing of the Fourth Edition, February 1996

Printed in the United States of America

Also available from Henry Strobel or your bookseller:

Violin Maker's Notebook	ISBN 0-9620673-3-4
The Health of the Violin, Viola, and Cello	ISBN 0-9620673-4-2
Art & Method of the Violin Maker	ISBN 0-9620673-5-0
Violin Making, Step by Step	ISBN 0-9620673-6-9
Cello Making, Step by Step	ISBN 0-9620673-7-7

PREFACE TO THE SECOND (REVISED) EDITION

The first edition, published with some reservations, was surprisingly well received. Rather than simply reprint it, I wanted to make a few needed changes and add some further measurements, clarifying notes, and drawings. For example, I revised the bass bridge spacing, and added a cello diagram and bridge templates for small instruments. Minor changes were made to various values in the tables where it was felt that the new value was better or more typical. The number of words in the "dictionary" was doubled and a true cross-reference added. The text was reviewed and expanded throughout.

The book is unchanged in essentials, a convenient, comprehensive, working reference. The master violin maker may not derive much new inspiration in his area of specialization. Others will find it very useful, especially in areas outside their normal experience. To the extent that it gives specific single values it attempts an impossible task; no one value is always optimum. To give an "acceptable range" of values would be equally flawed. The optimum value of a variable depends on others, the relationship of which I have tried to explain in some cases, but the final determination must be left to the perception and judgment of the violin maker in the context of a particular instrument.

No one has expressed an objection to the exclusive use of metric measures, U.S. violin makers having recognized their convenience and universality.

Thanks to all those who offered helpful suggestions for this second edition.

November 1988

PREFACE TO THE FIRST EDITION

The material presented here was originally compiled in 1984 for use in my violin workshop. Since then, I have continuously used, revised, and added to it.

This is not a book on the violin making process itself (of which there are sufficient), nor on specific repair techniques (of which there are too few). It does provide, compactly and conveniently, most of the basic SIZE and ADJUSTMENT data needed for working on instruments of the violin family.

The material presented, while simple in appearance, represents a substantial effort in research and validation. This is basic factual information, not magic formulae, pet theories, "how-to hints", or rhapsodies on old varnish. I do not presume to set myself up as an authority. Many readers will have more experience and training. However, this useful information is not readily available in similar form elsewhere.

Chapter 1 is on full size, Chapter 2 on smaller instruments. Chapter 3 just grew, a paragraph at a time, to include brief notes on many things.

Chapter 4 is on those "early" or unusual bowed instruments that the violin maker may encounter.
Out of my collection of books on the violin and violin making, several appeared to be (more or less) relevant and reliable. These are listed alphabetically, with comments, in the bibliography in Chapter 5.

In Chapter 6, Maker's Addendum, and in the Afterword, I allowed myself a more personal point of view.

Your suggestions for future editions are welcome.

HAS Oregon (July) 1988
For Henry Jr., Marguerite, and George

TABLE OF CONTENTS

PREFACES 5

Frontispiece 8

Chapter 1. STANDARD SIZE INSTRUMENTS
Introduction 9
Table of Useful Measurements 10
Remarks on the Table 11
Bridge and Fingerboard Templates 12
Bow Measurements 13

Chapter 2. OTHER INSTRUMENT SIZES
Introduction 14
Table of Violin Sizes 16
Table of Viola Sizes 16
Table of Cello Sizes 17
Table of Bass Sizes 17
Bridge Templates for Small Instruments 18

Chapter 3. NOTES ON VARIOUS SUBJECTS
Introduction 19
Tuning 19
Strings 19
The Bridge 21
Standard Violin Diagram 22
Standard Cello Diagram 22
The Sound Post 23
Measuring the Post Position 23
The Bass Bar 24
Wolf Tones 24
The Double Bass 24
Common Fiddle Faults 25
Factory Fiddles 25
Plywood Cellos and Basses 25

Chapter 4. SOME HISTORICAL AND OTHER BOWED
INSTRUMENTS
The Baroque Violin 26
Viola d'Amore 27
The Viol Family 27
Historical Note 28
The New Violin "Octet" 28
Miscellaneous Others 29

Chapter 5. FURTHER REFERENCE
Introduction 31
Bibliography 31
Periodicals 33
"Term Translator" 33
Violinist's "Notes" 37

Chapter 6. MAKER'S ADDENDUM

Introduction 38
Measuring Tools 38
Table of Additional Measurements 40
Graduation 41
Varnish 42
Wood 42
Glue 43
Graduation Control 43

AFTERWORD
Making and Repair 44
New and Old 45
About the Author 45
Notes 46
About the Book . . . . Back Cover

The drawing reproduced here by kind permission of the artist, Fritz Eichenberg, was an illustration for *Fiddler's Folly*, Robert H. Schauffler, 1942.

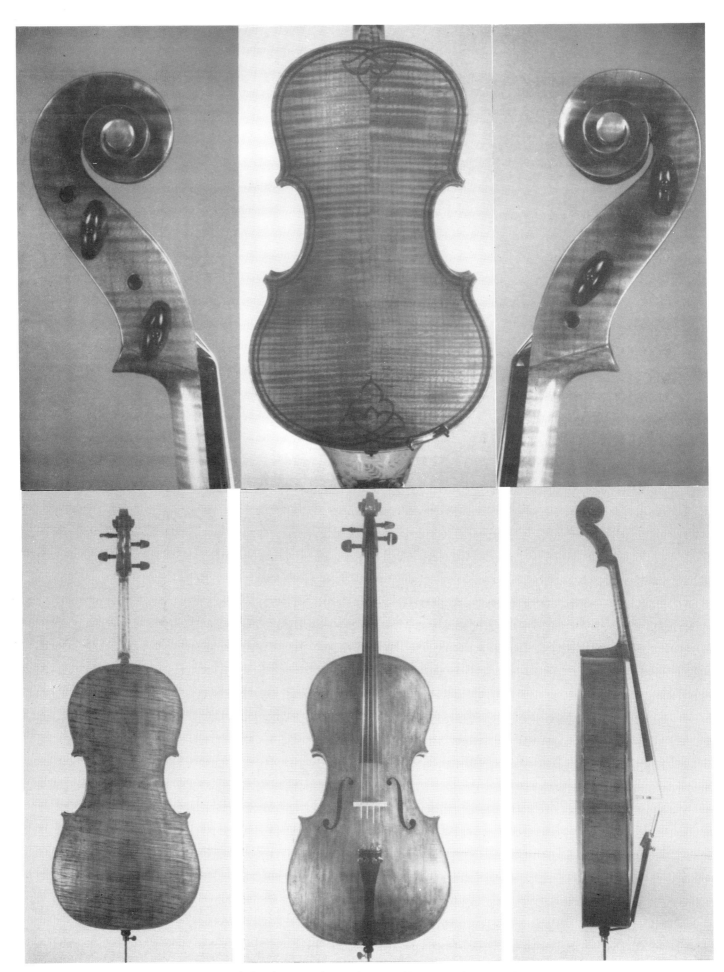

A Viola (upper) and a Cello by the Author

CHAPTER 1

STANDARD SIZE INSTRUMENTS

INTRODUCTION

It is part of the paradox of the violin that all its makers work within limits of size, shape, color, etc., such that unless one is a player, maker, or connoisseur, all violins look and sound more or less alike. Yet to a person familiar with violins, each has its own personality (voice, feel, and appearance) just as human singers do.

There is room for subtle style and sound differences, but every competent violin maker works to ACCEPTED STANDARDS of adjustment and dimensions, whether in new making or repair in order to satisfy the needs of the player. First, the basic standards must be met, which are the same for all players, and then perhaps minor adjustments to suit the individual performer.

This presentation deals only with the basic standards required by all players. It does not tell how to cut a bridge for a certain tone, or how to set a post to satisfy a particular musician; the finer adjustments can be achieved only by experience, patience, and insight. They are more in the category of tone (acoustic) adjustments rather than playability adjustments, the principal subject here. Tone adjustments tend to be somewhat subjective and problematic. The violin maker is often asked what happens if a particular change is made. He must frequently try to answer this question in the case of a particular instrument he is working on, but it cannot be answered generally (or in a book) because of all the other variables involved.

The standardization of playability adjustments does not exclude artistic individuality in violin making, but it does establish an essential common ground.

The violin maker is not a machine, calibrated for a production run, but an ARTIST giving individual expression to each instrument within the accepted limits. He has to determine each time the dimensions of each detail of the instrument. For these measurements two kinds of reference are used: numeric measurements, and direct patterns or gauges. Each maker provides his own patterns and gauges according to his needs and methods. (One will measure every detail; another will carve freehand.)

As an aid in making these patterns, and as a convenient numeric REFERENCE, I compiled for my own use the "Table of Useful Measurements" on the next page and the "Table of Additional Measurements" on pages 40 and 41. In doing so, I tried to compare, select, and reconcile (as far as practical) the information from various sources, and from my own experience.

The measurements given in these tables and in the tables of other sizes in Chapter 2 are not the rigid answer, but a reasonable starting point. The final criteria are always "Is it easy to play, and does it sound good?"

TABLE OF USEFUL MEASUREMENTS

MEASUREMENTS IN MM STANDARD SIZE INSTRUMENTS	VIOLIN 4/4	VIOLA 15½in	VIOLA 16½in	CELLO 4/4	BASS 3/4
Body Length, Approximate	356	394	419	755	1110
Upper Edge of Top to Bridge Center	195	210	225	400	610
Neck Length, Upper Edge of Top to Nut	130	140	150	280	425
Neck Thickness, Upper, Excluding FB	13	13.5	14	17	22
Neck Thickness, Lower, Excluding FB	14	14.5	15	19	30
Neck Thickness, Upper, Including FB	19	19.5	20.5	29	34
Neck Thickness, Lower, Including FB	21	21.5	22.5	33	41
Neck Height over Top Edge (Page 22)	6.0	8.0	9.0	19	25
(Violin E Side 0.7 lower, or: reduce fingerboard 0.7 on E side. See *Violin Making, Step by Step, page 58.*)					
Neck Heel Measurement (See page 22.)	26	27.5	28	42	66
Fingerboard Length	270	290	305	580	850
Fingerboard Width at Nut	23.5	24	25	31	42
Fingerboard Width at Lower End	42	45	46	63	87
Fingerboard Thickness on Sides	5.0	5.0	5.5	7.5	10
FB Surface Concavity under String 1	0.5	0.7	0.7	0.9	1.6
FB Surface Concavity under String 4	0.7	0.9	0.9	1.5	2.5
FB Surface Radius of Curvature	42	38	38	62	95
FB Flat Surface under String 4	---	See next page.		9X22	11X25
FB Height Projected to Bridge	27	31	32	81	150
String Length, Nut to Top of Bridge	330	356	380	695	1060
String Length, Bridge to Tailpiece	55	60	68	120	200
String 1-4 Spacing at Nut	16.3	16.5	17	22	30
(Divide into three equal parts along arc to locate strings 2 and 3.)					
String 1-4 Spacing at Bridge	33.5	37	38	47	80
String to String Spacing at Bridge	11.5	12.5	13	16.5	28
String 1 FB Clearance, Gut	3.5	4.0	4.5	5.5	11
String 1 FB Clearance, Steel	2.5	3.0	3.5	4.0	7.0
(Perlon symphony or steel rhythm bass 8.5)					
String 4 FB Clearance, Gut	5.5	6.0	6.5	8.0	16
String 4 FB Clearance, Steel	4.0	4.5	5.0	6.5	8.7
(Perlon symphony or steel rhythm bass 11)					
(Please see "string CLEARANCE" on page 20.)					
String Clearance at Nut (See page 20.)	About 1/3 the String Diameter				
(But not less than about 0.25 for violin or 0.55 for cello)					
String 2 Angle over Bridge, Degrees (See page 21.)	158	158	158	153	148
String Groove Depth at Nut and Bridge	About 1/3 the String Diameter				
String Groove Width at Nut and Bridge	About the String Diameter				
Bridge Thickness at Strings	1.3	1.4	1.5	2.6	4.5
Bridge Thickness at Feet	4.2	5.0	5.5	11	21
Saddle Height (See also page 40.)	Variable to Adjust the String Angle				
Sound Post Diameter	6.0	6.0	7.0	11	17
Peg Hole Spacing, Strings 1-4 and 2-3	15	18	18	27	--
Peg Hole Spacing, Strings 1-3	20	26	26	37	--
Pegbox to Inside Edge of Thumbpiece	16	17	17	28	--

TO CHANGE MM TO INCHES, DIVIDE BY 25.4

NOTE: Chapter 2 has TABLES for OTHER SIZES. Chapter 3 explains ADJUSTMENTS in more detail. Chapter 6 has ADDITIONAL information for the MAKER.

REMARKS ON THE TABLE

The table just presented gives reference measurements that primarily affect STANDARDIZATION and PLAYABILITY rather than acoustics or esthetics.

The violin maker is assumed to have acquired or developed outlines, patterns, molds, tools, and methods. The table excludes arching, graduation, bass bar and sound post fitting, and bridge cutting. However, they are treated briefly in Chapters 3 and 6.
Another point: in working from published drawings, it is sometimes unclear whether the measurement was intended along the arching or strings, or from the plan projection, whether the drawing was rescaled in reproduction or whether the original was accurately drawn. (Note that the string length is longer than the sum of the neck length and stop.) The professional maker will adapt his own templates from good models.

Some of the measurements are more IMPORTANT, such as string clearance, upper edge of top to bridge center ("stop"), neck length and thickness, and fingerboard projection (height projected to the bridge). Some others are less critical. Measurements are given in mm (and tenths in some cases). Of course, dimensions cannot be controlled to a tenth of a mm in wood. The measurements given are typical or design center values. It is not practical to state the range of acceptable variations, which depends on the model and related variables. Cellos, for example, often have a stop of 405 mm instead of the "idealized" 400 shown here, and thus a string length closer to 700 mm than 695.

The VIOLIN is the most highly standardized of the string instruments. VIOLAS and BASSES are quite variable. My table shows two very different viola samples. The maker as artist should appreciate the opportunity for originality provided by the viola.

Bridge heights are not given here. They are determined by the string clearance at the end of the fingerboard (after the fingerboard projection has been verified or corrected). One standard height is not always optimum. See THE BRIDGE in Chapter 3.

I have not included a height for the FINGERBOARD over the top, although this is often used (20 mm is usual for the violin). This depends on the arching and on the height of the neck over the top edge; it is far more reliable to use the fingerboard height extended to the bridge using a straight edge (or an L- shaped gauge).

Nominal RADII of curvature are given, but the fingerboard is often given a varied curvature, less curved on the treble side. The FLAT surface under string 4 of the cello and bass is approx. 60 degrees from the vertical. Also, older violas may have a flat surface under the C string, about 7x12 mm and a 42 mm radius.

The longitudinal surface CONCAVITY is greatest not at the center of the fingerboard length, but at that of the vibrating string. Ideally this concavity is less for steel strings.

To complement the table, I have included a copy of my bridge and fingerboard TEMPLATES on the next page. These are typical, but will not be optimum for all archings, models, and player preferences.

Please see Chapter 3 for more detailed information.

BRIDGE AND FINGERBOARD TEMPLATES

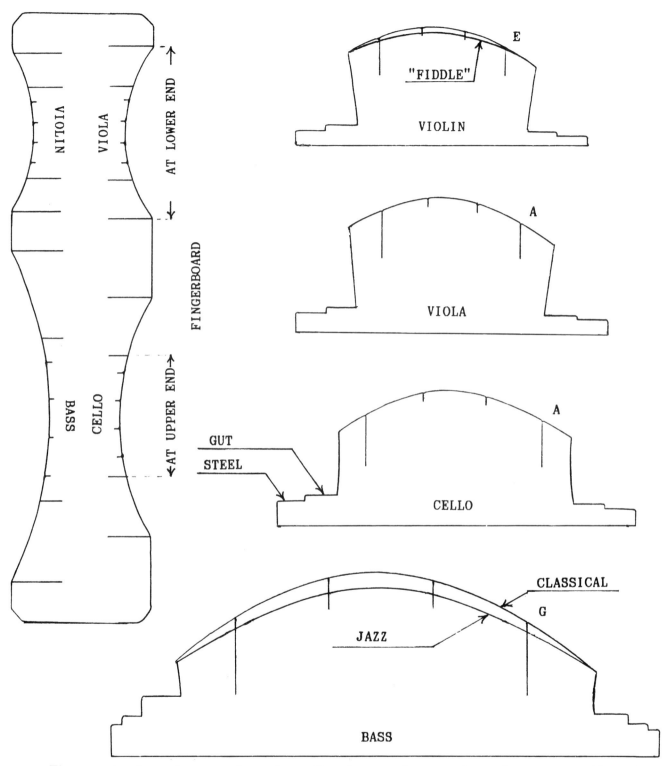

These are tracings of my wood templates. (See the note about metal templates on page 18.) String clearance gauges should be checked with calipers against the table on page 10. IMPORTANT: See also "string CLEARANCE", page 20.

The fingerboard template checks the nominal radius of curvature and string spacing at the nut. See pages 10, 11 for the FLAT surface under string 4 of the cello and bass fingerboards.

The string to string spacing for a 5 string bass may be less than 28 mm depending on the width of the fingerboard and bridge blank.

BOW MEASUREMENTS

The three principal bow measurements, overall LENGTH, WEIGHT, and BALANCE point from the frog, are not standardized. These are ultimately the choice of the performer or instructor, based on personal requirements and preferences.

Other important bow characteristics, STIFFNESS of the stick, and thus the TENSION that can be applied to the hair, are not usually measured objectively, but are very noticeable to the player.

The bow lengths listed in the tables of Chapter 2 are primarily intended for the identification of fractional sized bows.

VIOLIN bows range from about 728 to 752 mm overall, but most modern ones are about 745 mm.

Authorities often give the VIOLA bow length as slightly shorter than the violin bow; they are in the same range, however. The viola bow is generally heavier and stiffer.

The table below shows measurements in mm for full size bows. These are only representative and do not indicate the acceptable range. Balance points especially have a wide range; they can also be moved somewhat by choice of fittings, wrapping, tip loading, etc. in the finished bow. BASS bows vary widely. The samples given are not necessarily recommended.

The balance point is given as its distance in front of the frog in the forward (loosened) position.

BOW TYPE	LENGTH OVERALL	WEIGHT (GRAMS)	BALANCE POINT	FROG LENGTH	FERRULE WIDTH	BUTTON LENGTH
VIOLIN	745	60	185	45	13.5	16
VIOLA	740	70	195	48	14	16
CELLO	715	80	170	51	15	18
BASS, FRENCH	725	125	140	68	18	30
BASS, GERMAN	750	150	120	70	19	60

TO CHANGE GRAMS TO OUNCES, DIVIDE BY 28.4.

CAMBER of the bow: When the average, non-tensioned violin or viola bow is placed hair-down on a flat surface, the stick should touch or nearly touch the hair. Otherwise it needs respringing. (Stiffer bows, and cello and bass bows may have a greater separation.) The stick should be nearest to the hair about 5/8 of the way from the frog end.

With the frog fully forward, the HAIR should be just slack enough to allow for the shrinking from decreases in humidity, and the GRIP should be within a mm of of the front of the frog.

Two BOOKS on BOW MAKING, those of Bolander and Henderson, are listed in the Bibliography, page 31.

Chapter 2

OTHER INSTRUMENT SIZES

INTRODUCTION

STANDARD SIZED instruments were tabulated in Chapter 1 and are all full sized (4/4), except the 3/4 bass. With the exception of the 4/4 bass, all the "other" instrument sizes are smaller than full size.

The SMALLER instruments have traditionally been given fractional designations. These evolved haphazardly and were never standardized. 4/4 violins are quite standard at about 356 mm or 14 inches in body length, but have ranged from about 350 to 365.

A widely accepted schedule of TRADITIONAL SIZES was published by Metropolitan Music, tabulating all major dimensions in cm down to 1/64 for violin, and down to 1/8 for cello and bass. Scherl and Roth used this same tabulation in a decimal inch form.

A Lutherie Study Group in Cremona attempted to rationalize the series of small violins on a different mathematical basis. In it the small sizes shrink somewhat, the 1/16 approximating the more traditional 1/32 size.

Konrad Leonhardt presented a different series (GBM Standard 1978923), and in this the small sizes swell somewhat, the 1/16 (his smallest) approximating the more traditional 1/8 size.

(See the references in the Bibliography, Chapter 5, for the above sources.)

A SUZUKI violin series is similar to the traditional sizes, except that its 1/10 approximates the 1/16, and its 1/16 approximates the 1/32. See also the Suzuki note to the cello table on page 17.

A size schedule was given in the "The Instrumentalist" for May-June, 1950 by Christian Bryder, who was the violin expert at Lyon & Healy in Chicago. The Warren School used this. It agreed with the traditional sizes, but only went down to 1/4.

Then there are the MENC (Music Educators' National Conference) designations. These ("Standard, Intermediate, and Junior") are indicated along with the traditional designations in the tables on pages 16, 17. Or, one may try to avoid the issue of fractional size designations by referring to "a child's violin of (so many) mm", for example. Ultimately the instrument must be measured by the child.

Of course, the "new violin family" of the Catgut Acoustical Society is not considered in this context. But see NEW VIOLIN "OCTET" in Chapter 4.

After a painstaking analysis of the size schedules mentioned above and measurements of actual instruments, I derived realistic nominal BODY LENGTHS and rounded ranges of values to use in determining the nominal size. Body lengths between these ranges can be designated 7/8, 5/8, etc.

NOMINAL TRADITIONAL VIOLIN SIZES

SIZE	4/4	3/4	1/2	1/4	1/8	1/16	1/32
LENGTH	356	335	310	280	255	230	215
From	350	330	300	270	250	225	210
To	360	340	320	290	260	240	220

A useful APPROXIMATION is that most measurements decrease by about 8% for each downward step in the series 4/4, 3/4, 1/2, 1/4, 1/8, 1/16, 1/32. Thus, one can multiply the 4/4 value by 0.92 to approximate the 3/4 value, by 0.85 for the 1/2, 0.78 for 1/4, 0.72 for 1/8, 0.66 for 1/16, and by 0.61 for 1/32. To go up a step, as from 3/4 to 4/4, one can multiply by 1.09. This agrees within 3% with the nominal lengths above. Of course, all dimensions do not necessarily change in scale on all models. CELLO bows decrease in length about 6% for each downward step.

The TABLES on pages 16 and 17 do not provide construction information for these instruments; they do facilitate IDENTIFYING the nominal size of an instrument or bow, or of parts in inventory (bridges, tailpieces, etc.)

They also provide APPROXIMATE ADJUSTMENT information for the various sizes based on the 8% rule. Common sense and a basic knowledge of playing requirements will suffice to adapt the data given to a particular instrument. Selecting the correct BRIDGE BLANK is the essential starting point. A wider, narrower, or lower blank may be required by the instrument's width or fingerboard projection. If the f-holes are widely separated, the corresponding bar position requires a wider bridge. Full size bridge blanks are available in even mm widths: for viola about 46-52 (48 typical), for cello about 86-98 (90 typical), and for bass in various 4 and 5 stringed sizes, sometimes custom made. Finding the right model, size, and wood quality is sometimes a challenge.

One of the most important measurements is that of the FINGERBOARD PROJECTION ("FB Height Projected to Bridge"), since it may involve resetting the neck. Do not simply follow the tables; make sure that the projection will be right for the instrument and for the height of the bridge you want to use.

The purpose of the tables is to guide, not to complicate. Use the size of fitting that is practical, or available and appropriate. BAR dimensions are only a guide and depend on graduation and other acoustic considerations. The length of the bar can be approximated by 7/9 of the body length. The shape and height are more important than the precise length.

String spacing is measured from center to center, but string clearance is from the bottom of the string to the surface of the fingerboard. It is convenient to make CLEARANCE GAUGES as part of the BRIDGE TEMPLATES. APPROXIMATE bridge templates for the SMALLER instruments can be derived form these by proportional reduction. See page 18. It may be desirable to make bridges for young students slightly more curved and thicker at the top.

In violins and violas, the "STOP" (upper edge of the top to the bridge center) should be in the ratio 3 to 2 to the neck length (upper edge of the top to the nut). In cellos and many basses this ratio is 10 to 7. This varies, especially in basses, which are likely to be individual in many respects.

VIOLIN SIZES	4/4	3/4	1/2	1/4	1/8	1/16
MENC Designation	STD.	INT.	JUN.	---	---	---*
Body Length, Nominal	356	335	310	280	255	230
String Length, Nominal	330	310	285	260	235	215
Bow Length, Nominal, Overall	745	690	630	550	500	450
Bridge Blank Width at Feet	41	38	35	32	29	27
Bridge Thickness at Feet	4.2	3.9	3.6	3.3	3.0	2.8
Bridge Thickness at Strings	1.3	1.2	1.1	1.0	0.9	0.9
Sound Post Diameter	6.0	6.0	5.0	5.0	4.0	4.0
Bar Length	277	260	241	218	198	179
Bar Width	5.5	5.1	4.7	4.3	3.9	3.6
Bar Height at Bridge	12	11	10	9.4	8.6	7.9
String 1-4 Spacing at Nut	16.3	15	14	13	12	11
String 1-4 Spacing at Bridge	33.5	31	29	26	24	22
String 1 FB Clearance, Gut	3.5	3.2	3.0	2.7	2.5	2.3
String 1 FB Clearance, Steel	2.5	2.3	2.1	1.9	1.8	1.6
String 4 FB Clearance, Gut	5.5	5.1	4.7	4.3	3.9	3.6
String 4 FB Clearance, Steel	4.0	3.7	3.4	3.1	2.9	2.6
FB Height Projected to Bridge	27	25	24	22	20	19
Fingerboard Length	270	250	230	210	195	180
Tailpiece Length	114	105	95	89	82	75
Pegbox to Peg Thumbpiece	16	15	14	13	11	10
Peg Thumbpiece Width	22	21	20	19	18	17

* Suzuki 1/10, 1/16, approximate the traditional 1/16, 1/32.

Approximate:	17 in	16 in	15 ½ in	14 in	13 in	12 in
VIOLA SIZES	LARGE	MED.	SMALL	3/4	1/2	1/4
MENC Designation	STD.	STD.	STD.	INT.*	JUN.*	MINI*
Body Length, Nominal	430	410	390	356	335	310
String Length, Nominal	390	375	355	(See	(See	(See
Bow Length, Nominal, Overall	750	740	740	4/4	3/4	1/2
Bridge Blank Width at Feet	50-52	48-50	46-50	vn.)	vn.)	vn.)
Bridge Thickness at Feet	5.5	5.3	5.0			
Bridge Thickness at Strings	1.5	1.5	1.4			
Sound Post Diameter	7.0	7.0	6.0			
Bar Length	334	319	303			
Bar Width	6.6	6.3	6.0			
Bar Height at Bridge	15	14	13			
String 1-4 Spacing at Nut	17	17	16.5			
String 1-4 Spacing at Bridge	38	37	36			
String 1 FB Clearance, Gut	4.5	4.3	4.0			
String 1 FB Clearance, Steel	3.5	3.3	3.0			
String 4 FB Clearance, Gut	6.5	6.3	6.0			
String 4 FB Clearance, Steel	5.0	4.8	4.5			
FB Height Projected to Bridge	32	31	30			
Fingerboard Length	305	300	290			
Tailpiece Length	135	130	125			
Pegbox to Peg Thumbpiece	18	17	17			
Peg Thumbpiece Width	25	24	24			

* May be 4/4, 3/4, 1/2 violins specially strung. True violas (wider and deeper bodies) are preferable.

CELLO SIZES	4/4	3/4	1/2	1/4	1/8
MENC Designation	STD.	INT.	JUN.	---*	---*
Body Length, Nominal	755	690	650	580	530
String Length, Nominal	695	635	600	535	490
Bow Length, Nominal, Overall	715	670	630	590	560
Bridge Blank Width at Feet	90	83	77	70	65
Bridge Thickness at Feet	11	10	9.3	8.6	7.9
Bridge Thickness at Strings	2.6	2.4	2.2	2.0	1.9
Sound Post Diameter	11	10	9.0	9.0	8.0
Bar Length	587	536	505	451	412
Bar Width	11	10	9.5	8.5	8.0
Bar Height at Bridge	25	23	21	19	18
String 1-4 Spacing at Nut	22	20	19	17	16
String 1-4 Spacing at Bridge	47	43	40	37	34
String 1 FB Clearance, Gut	5.5	5.1	4.7	4.3	3.9
String 1 FB Clearance, Steel	4.0	3.7	3.4	3.1	2.9
String 4 FB Clearance, Gut	8.0	7.4	6.8	6.3	5.7
String 4 FB Clearance, Steel	6.5	6.0	5.5	5.1	4.7
FB Height Projected to Bridge	81	75	69	63	58
Fingerboard Length	580	530	500	450	410
Tailpiece Length	235	215	200	180	160
Pegbox to Peg Thumbpiece	28	26	24	22	20
Peg Thumbpiece Width	38	36	34	32	30

* Suzuki 1/2, 1/4, approximate the traditional 1/4, 1/8. Suzuki 1/8, 1/10 are about 455, 400 mm long. (A viola with an end pin has also been used.)

BASS SIZES	4/4	3/4	1/2	1/4
MENC Designation	---	STD.	INT.	JUN.*
Body Length, Nominal	1160	1110	1020	940
String Length, Nominal	1100	1060	975	900
Bow Length, French, Overall	725	725	675	675
Bow Length, German, Overall	750	750	710	710
Bridge Blank Width at Feet	160	150	138	127
Bridge Thickness at Feet	23	21	19	18
Bridge Thickness at Strings	4.9	4.5	4.2	3.8
Sound Post Diameter	18	17	16	15
Bar Length	932	855	792	726
Bar Width	25	23	21	19
Bar Height at Bridge	44	40	37	34
String 1-4 Spacing at Nut	33	30	28	25
String 1-4 Spacing at Bridge	87	80	74	68
String 1 FB Clearance, Gut	12	11	10	9.3
String 1 FB Clearance, Steel	7.6	7.0	6.5	5.9
String 4 FB Clearance, Gut	17	16	15	14
String 4 FB Clearance, Steel	9.5	8.7	8.0	7.4
FB Height Projected to Bridge	160	150	138	127
Fingerboard Length	890	850	780	730
Tailpiece Length	350	340	310	290
(Tuning "Machines")	—	—	—	—

* A cello is sometimes tuned an octave above the bass for children.

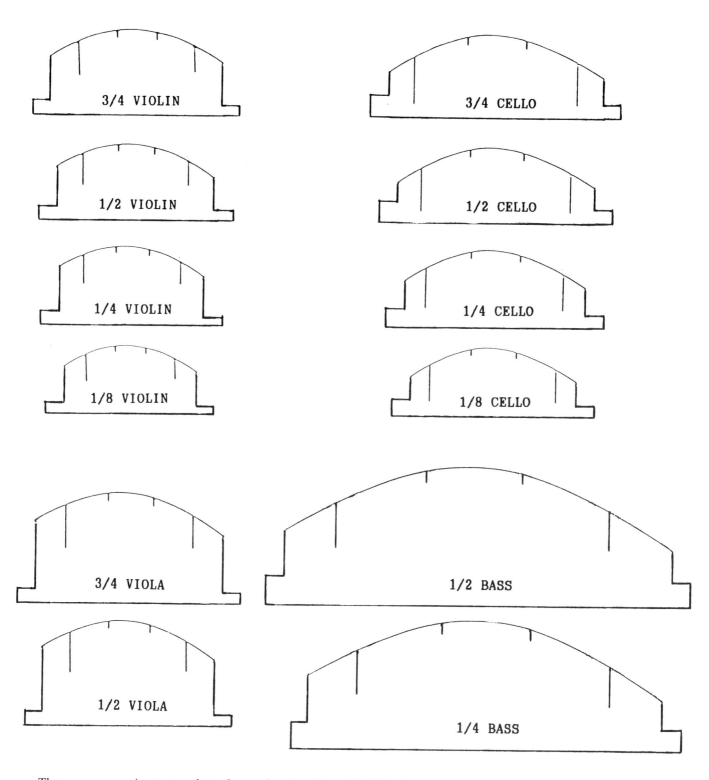

These are approximate templates for steel strings from the 8% rule. As always the final setup is determined by the characteristics of the instrument and strings and the needs of the player. The templates may be made of aluminum, about 1 mm thick. Slots may be cut at the string 1 and 4 positions to allow marking the bridge blank for preliminary cutting. Fingerboard radii could also be derived from the 8% rule (see APPROXIMATION on page 15), but in practice this is not done, small fingerboards having very little more curvature than full size ones. Check gauges with calipers against the tables on pages 16-17.

NOTES ON VARIOUS SUBJECTS

INTRODUCTION

The intent of the brief notes in this chapter is to provide basic facts without being too obvious, dogmatic, or conjectural. Subjective statements about tone are excluded, as are mathematical definitions and lengthy rationales. I hope it is a practical overview to the items covered.

TUNING

The numeric suffixes below refer to the octave number as on the piano (page 46). For example, A4 is in the 4th octave, which begins with middle C. An A440 tuning fork is the usual reference.

STRING NUMBER (FROM RIGHT)	4	3	2	1
VIOLIN (Treble Clef)	G3	D4	A4	E5
VIOLA (Alto Clef)	C3	G3	D4	A4
CELLO (Bass Clef)	C2	G2	D3	A3
BASS (Standard or "Orchestra" Tuning)	E1	A1	D2	G2
BASS ("Solo" Tuning)	F#1	B1	E2	A2

Tuning the bass requires the use of harmonics (page 46). Or, a hands-free electronic tuner is convenient in the shop. The range of the standard BASS can be extended down to C1 by a mechanical extension of the E1 string, or down to B1 or C1 by the addition of a low fifth string. In other cases, the range can be extended upwards on a 5 stringed bass by a high C3 string in addition to the standard set. See also "FIDDLE", page 29.

STRINGS

Strings are made of plain GUT or STEEL, which may be wound with various metals, or of steel stranded "ROPE" or of synthetic fibers ("PERLON", nylon) which are always metal wound for bowed instruments. Steel strings are usually used on the small (student) instruments. They require fine TUNERS at the tailpiece (except the bass). The first string of the violin is always steel, as are often the upper (or all) strings of the larger full size instruments. Gut or perlon strings do not require fine tuners but some students use proprietary anti-slip pegs with them. Good perlon strings last longer and stay in tune far better than gut, but good gut strings are still preferred by many.

For a given tuning, the greater the TENSION, the louder. Also, for a given tuning, the heavier the string, the greater its tension. On small instruments, where the string length is short, the tension will be low unless heavier strings are used. See page 46. This is provided for by using the special strings made for SMALL INSTRUMENTS. It is also usually preferable to use a heavier C string on a small viola. However, lighter strings may be easier to play.

String GAUGE is simply the string diameter as read from a micrometer. It can also be expressed in the traditional Pirastro Measure, 20 times the mm reading. Or, one may halve the number of thousandths of an inch to approximate PM. Gauge itself does not determine the weight or tension, which depends on the kind of winding, etc. For example, a set of violin strings might be 5, 14, 17, and 16 PM for E, A, D, G, respectively. Note that the gauge makes a big increase from E to A (steel to gut), but decreases from D to G (aluminum to silver winding) because of the construction and heaviness of the material. Strings are labelled thin, medium, thick, stiff, or dolce, forte, etc.

The string CLEARANCE over the lower end of the fingerboard should be less for strings under greater tension, and vice versa. A taut string is hard to finger if too high and will sharpen; a slacker string will vibrate farther and buzz if too low. Thus, steel strings are given less clearance than perlon, perlon a little less than gut, and treble strings less than bass. Clearance may be made somewhat LESS than shown in the table on page 10, especially on cello and bass, if the curvature and concavity of the fingerboard are optimum and if no allowance is given for seasonal bridge height variations (or if adjusting screws are installed). For BASS, the clearance is sometimes reduced to 9 and 12 mm (gut), and 6 and 7.5 mm (steel) for strings 1 and 4, respectively.

For smooth tuning and long string service, the GROOVES in the nut and bridge must be free and smooth, no deeper than necessary to securely align the strings. They should be rounded downward toward the pegs at the nut and toward the tailpiece at the bridge, and blackened with a soft pencil (graphite). The nut must present a definite, non rounded, stop to the string at the fingerboard.

String clearance at the NUT is generally about 1/3 the string diameter, but should be not less than 0.25 mm, the thickness of an ordinary business card or violin E string for violin; for cello it should be not less than 0.55 mm. Strings should be easy to stop in the first position yet never buzz nor interfere with left hand pizzicato. This also depends on the fingerboard concavity near the nut. The string 1 groove at the nut should not be too close to the edge of the fingerboard; if necessary for secure fingering, the grooves may be shifted slightly toward the bass side. (Everything else being correct, this is not necessary.)

Various kinds of STRAIN RELIEF and "TONE FILTER" devices are supplied with some strings. They are intended to reduce string wear at the bridge, to prevent cutting into the bridge, or to dampen the higher harmonics and noise. With a bridge of hard wood and properly fitted grooves, they are often unnecessary. A triangular ebony insert is often used or, preferably, a small pad of parchment glued under the violin E string, the viola A and D strings, etc.

PEGS should be spaced as stated on page 10, and located to avoid strings rubbing on them. For ease of use and a graceful appearance their thumbpieces should be spaced from the side of the peg box as noted on page 10. The measurement given is to the thumbpiece itself, not the collar, of the peg. Occasionally the C and G viola peg POSITIONS are interchanged to decrease the bending and friction of the thick C at the nut. Likewise, the E and A machine screw positions on the bass are sometimes interchanged.

For ease of tuning, it is desirable to adjust the strings so the THUMBPIECES of the pegs are approximately vertical. Use only a standard commercial peg compound.
String HOLES in the pegs should be approximately in the center of the pegbox to allow a single layer winding ending near, but not against the side of the pegbox.

Strings should not loop around the TAILPIECE but go straight from its "fret" to the bridge. This length should be nominally 1/6 that of the string length from bridge to nut, about two octaves and a fifth higher. This will not be achieved in many cases because of string characteristics, fine tuners, attached mutes, available tailpieces, etc. In practice, this length is increased on the larger instruments as shown on page 10.

A related rule gives the length of the FINGERBOARD as 5/6 of the string length. Thus touching the cello A string at the end of the fingerboard sounds E5. This rule is followed only approximately in practice, especially on violas and basses. Unneeded extra length adds undesirable extra weight at the end of the fingerboard. A groove on its underside aids gluing and removal.

When shifting up, the thumb encounters the heel of the neck in the 5th position on the violin and viola, the 4th on the cello, and under D2 on the E string on the bass.

THE BRIDGE

Cutting the bridge produces effects too complex and interrelated to analyze or state simply. The mass and stiffness of various parts affect the timber and response. The violin maker exercises his artistic idiosyncrasies, of course, but more importantly his acoustic intuition based on experience and careful testing and listening. The THICKNESS of the upper part and the STIFFNESS of the legs and center are the most important adjustments.

The BACK of the bridge is flat, cut precisely on the quarter (some prefer the quartered surface on the front), and approximately perpendicular to the top of the instrument. More precisely, the center of the bridge should divide the string angle into two equal parts. The WIDTH of the bridge at the feet should fit the bass bar position. See BRIDGE BLANK, page 15 and BRIDGE FOOT, page 24.
The HEIGHT of the bridge affects tone, loudness, and playability. Also, a sharp string angle over the bridge puts a little more force downward on the top, a factor one might consider on old or delicate instruments with steel strings, which may have perhaps 25% more tension than gut. (Note that the downward force spreads the legs of the cello bridge somewhat, which must be considered in fitting its feet.)

As required by the string clearance values shown in the tables, the bridge is made higher for gut strings; it may also become too high when the HUMIDITY is high, necessitating a seasonal change of bridges, especially on cello and bass. Some bridges have screw adjustments for this. (Also to adapt between classical and jazz bass playing.)

The optimum string ANGLE will vary depending on the above factors and other characteristics of the instrument. The angles given in the table on page 10 are those formed by the 2nd string (about 158 degrees for the A string of a typical violin with a 33 mm high bridge and a Hill model tailpiece). If a string adjuster is used, the angle may vary depending on the type of adjuster and tailpiece thickness.

Note: Traditionally, some makers have made much of this angle. However, it is troublesome and probably unnecessary to measure it exactly. I no longer bother. If the other measurements and adjustments are OK, the string angle will also be satisfactory.

THEORETICALLY, the SET UP would proceed thus:
1. Bridge height at center set by instrument design and tone requirements.
2. Fingerboard projection (height extended to bridge) set by bridge height.
3. Fingerboard curvature and concavity set by requirements of fingering, bowing, and string type.
4. Bridge height at strings 1 and 4 set by string clearance requirements.
5. Bridge curvature (to locate strings 2 and 3) set by bowing requirements and corresponding to the end of the fingerboard.
6. Bridge cutting for fit and tone requirements.

PRACTICALLY, one usually:
1. Selects (or accepts) the fingerboard projection, curvature, and concavity.
2. Fits the bridge feet.
3. Locates strings 1 and 4 by string spacing and clearance requirements.
4. Sets the bridge curvature with a standard template.
5. Locates strings 2 and 3 along the curve with the template or dividers.   6. Completes acoustical and artistic adjustments to top, thickness, edges, feet, and cutouts of bridge.

Bridge height and string angle can be adjusted by varying the FINGERBOARD PROJECTION at the bridge, the height of the NECK over the top, and the SADDLE height. See the diagram below. The neck height over the top edge and/or the saddle may also have to be increased for fingerboard and/or tailpiece clearance in violins with very full or abrupt arching.

The question of how static forces affect the tone is complicated. But stresses should not be built in (such as forcing ribs into line), and downward bridge force should be balanced with the top and bar strength to avoid deformation.

STANDARD VIOLIN DIAGRAM

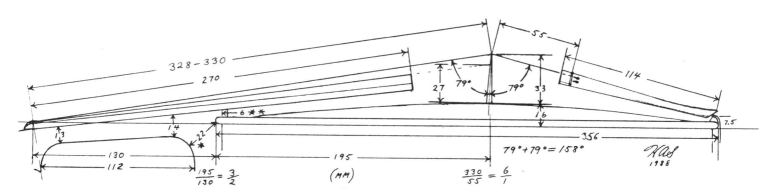

STANDARD CELLO DIAGRAM

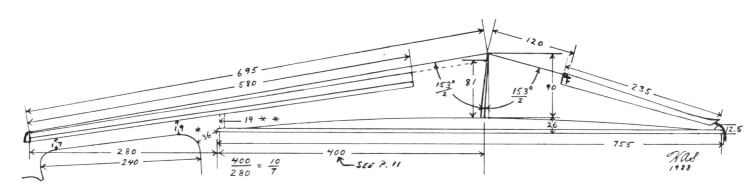

* If measured obliquely with dividers from the edge of the top to the center line of the heel, the values on page 10 apply, 26 mm on violin, 42 on cello.
** The neck height over the top edge is measured from the highest point on the edge vertically to the fingerboard, not at the end of the neck.

THE SOUND POST

The standard or initial POSITION of the post is in line with the center of the right foot of the bridge, vertical, with a space of about half the post diameter between the back edge of the bridge foot and the front edge of the post. It should be long enough (tight enough) to just stand securely with the strings slack, and fitted precisely to the inside arching of the top and back.

Various interrelated tone and playability changes occur when the post is moved relative to the bridge or its length is changed. The violin maker acquires a "feel" for this. He also is careful to maintain the fit of the post to top and back. Otherwise the tone is affected, and the top may be damaged. The TIGHTNESS also varies with humidity; a seasonal sound post adjustment may be necessary.

Given the above initial setting, the post is first moved relative to the bridge foot. Usually, the post may be moved LENGTHWISE of the violin without changing its fit or length. This has little effect on tightness, but it does modify the tone qualities, especially of the upper strings. The best position will often be closer to the bridge in an instrument with a thin top. Moving the post closer to the bridge usually gives a more intense, bright tone, farther away, more mellow or soft. (Here I cannot avoid a verbal description of tone.) The post should remain vertical when seen from the side, looking across the instrument.

When the post is moved LATERALLY (nearer the bar or nearer the right f-hole), the effect is more complicated since both the position and tightness change at the same time. If the post was too tight, moving it toward the bar allows free vibration of the lower register and "evens out" the strings. But if the post is shortened and then moved toward the f-hole (without getting tighter), the lower register may be favored again because a larger area of the top is affected by the action of the bridge pivoting over the post. The final lateral setting is often in line with the outside part of the bridge foot, somewhat like that of the bar. (See the next page.)

Once the best position is found, it may be advantageous to leave the top end of the post undisturbed and to make minor seasonal tightness adjustments by a very small lateral adjustment of the bottom of the post. (A large movement would require refitting the post.) Note that in looking at the post through the upper eye of the f-hole, the slope of the arching makes the bottom of the post appear closer to the rib. This effect is not present when looking through the end pin hole. It is advisable to slacken the strings before moving the top of the post to avoid damage to the spruce. (In the larger instruments this is a practical necessity.)

MEASURING THE POST POSITION

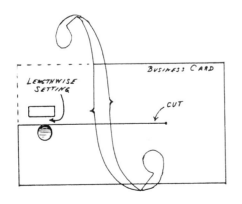
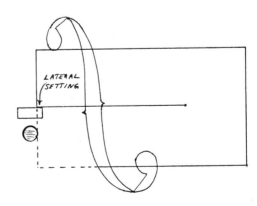

THE BASS BAR

Fitting the bar is critical for tone and is part of the top tuning process. "SPRINGING the bar" is not desirable of itself since it builds in a temporary stress. The wood does not "wear out", but the bar may become slightly flattened over time; thus replacement bars are usually sprung slightly to help preserve the arching. Thin old tops may need a stiffer bass bar.

The bar is not centered under the BRIDGE FOOT, but is approximately under the outside half of the bridge foot. (See Bridge Foot Extension past the Bar, page 41.) Its ANGLE is determined by taking 1/7 of the distance from the center to the edge at both the upper and lower maximum widths of the top. The maximum HEIGHT is under the bridge. (Or, as some makers prefer, at the center of the bar.) See pages 15 and 40 for determination of the bar LENGTH.

The bar is trimmed to achieve the desired "TAP TONE"; the top is held near the upper side edge (technically at a node of vibration mode 5) and tapped with a finger in the center. A clear "ring" is thought to indicate a balanced, well graduated top. REBARRING is sometimes elective, like rehairing or tonsillectomy. But it may also be quite necessary, as when the bar is too low, resulting in a "flabby" G string.

WOLF TONES

The wolf occurs when a strong body vibration interferes with the string vibration. It is frequently found at the second finger, first position on the second string, and on the same note in higher positions on the lower strings. It is more likely to be severe in cellos (around F on the G string). It is caused by design anomalies, some parts being too heavy, others too thin. It may appear as a PULSATION, ROUGHNESS OR JUMP IN FREQUENCY; it should not be confused with rattles at certain notes caused by loose glue joints, etc. It is less severe in more highly arched instruments. Too thin a top or too heavy a fingerboard may aggravate it. (Excess wood should be removed from the bottom of the fingerboard, as a general rule.) Adjusting the post, a stiffer bar, or lighter strings may help. Several kinds of "WOLF ELIMINATOR" are found, ranging from the makeshift wine bottle cork wedged under the tailpiece to those described here. One is a weight (usually a BRASS TUBE on the third string) between bridge and tailpiece, which is used to tune this string section to the wolf note. The frequency is lowest when midway between bridge and tailpiece. It is raised by moving nearer the bridge, or lowered further by increasing the weight. Use no more weight than necessary. A much more effective and less troublesome type is a small mechanical RESONATOR glued to the inside of the top; commercial units are made in the ranges D-E, Eb-F, and E-F#. Its position is first determined experimentally by sticking it to the outside of the top with a very little "putty" about 45 mm below the left f-hole. The effect is least at the rib and increases as it is moved toward the strings. A good, responsive cello with a wolf can be made a great cello by a properly fitted resonator, but avoid over correction.

THE DOUBLE BASS

Like the viola, the bass is not well standardized. A descendant of the double bass viol and tuned in fourths, it also has peculiarities of construction, sloping shoulders and back bracing in the flat-backed (not the cello) style, outside "linings" (cornices) and, of course, machine screw tuning. The information in the table on page 10 is for the standard, 3/4 bass. Larger basses, small chamber basses, different tunings, string extensions, 5 string versions, and high saddles may be encountered. This last is intended to reduce the downward bridge force with steel strings on antique basses, or to correct the string angle if the neck was installed incorrectly. Basses, especially "full size" are quite variable in model and measurements. There is also a wider range of bows than the table on page 17 indicates.

COMMON FIDDLE FAULTS

We are addressing here primarily design or adjustment faults, not repair techniques.

On old or non-standard violins:
> An incorrect neck length or poorly placed f-hole notches.
> Inadequate neck height over the top edge. (A shim at the button, or, if the neck is too thin, under the fingerboard.)

On neglected or mistreated violins:
> A warped bridge or a low fingerboard. (The neck should be reset rather than wedge the fingerboard.)
> Sound post cracks or sunken top. (May require a plaster cast and an inlaid patch with tapered edges.)
> F-hole cracks, other cracks and openings, eroded top edges.
> Top worked too thin.
> Fingerboard needs planing, or was incorrectly planed.

On poorly made violins:
> A thick neck, "clubby" heel, or scroll drooping below the nut.
> Too heavily built.
> "Plastic" glue or varnish.

On poorly repaired or "unadjusted" violins:
> Too high a nut, sharp edges on nut or fingerboard, poorly fitted bridges, or too long a tailpiece fastener.
> Top too thin, crude repairs, or wrong glue.
> Sound post jammed in tightly or otherwise poorly fitted.

FACTORY FIDDLES

For 150 years or so these have proliferated, good and bad. The worst may have no corner blocks, integral bass bar, no linings, painted purfling and faked wood grain (sometimes artistic), machine pressed and ungraduated arching, with tone to match.

The best are fine student instruments; the worst should be destroyed. The rest constitute the mediocre majority.

Most modern mass produced instruments are dimensionally correct, at least externally but some student violins are very "woody". These heavily sprayed, machine routed fiddles are essentially ungraduated with thick plates and the consequent uninspiring tone. This effect is unfortunately magnified in the smaller violins. However, regraduation is usually not economically justified on these.

PLYWOOD CELLOS & BASSES

Lamination cuts production cost and provides resistance to cracking; thus it finds wide use in student instruments. It entails certain problems in repair and adjustment, and falls short on artistic grounds. (The same might be said of fiber glass bows, but a good fiber glass bow is preferable to a mediocre wood bow.)

Chapter 4

SOME HISTORICAL AND OTHER
BOWED INSTRUMENTS

BAROQUE VIOLIN

This is the violin as it was before the early 19th century changes involving higher pitch, greater string tension, and a longer neck. Modern violins are occasionally converted to baroque for the performance of music with instruments "authentic" to the period of composition, and usually at a slightly lower pitch. A pre-Tourte outcurved bow is also used.

The major differences are as follows. The fingerboard is shorter, flatter, lighter (not solid ebony), and wedge shaped (thicker at the body). The neck is shorter and attached flush and nearly perpendicularly to the ribs with a heavier heel. The tailpiece is shorter and lighter, the bar shorter and lower, the sound post thinner, the bridge flatter, lower, and of a more archaic design. A chin rest was not used originally.

Access to good models is essential for the maker. The Hill and Sacconi books in the Bibliography are good references. Strings are all gut, plain for the upper, "rope" for the lower.

TYPICAL MEASUREMENTS COMPARED	MODERN	BAROQUE
Neck Length, Upper Edge of Top to NUT	130	123
Fingerboard Length	270	215
Fingerboard Width at Nut	23.5	25.5
Fingerboard Width at Lower End	42	40
FB Surface Radius of Curvature	42	52
Bridge Height	33	29
Sound Post Diameter	6	5
Bar Width	5.5	4.5
Bar Height at Bridge	11	7
Bar Length	270	240

(I recently converted a baroque violin back to modern condition for a customer. It was of the Turin school, about 1750, and had of course been "modernized" in the 19th century. Several years ago it had been changed back to baroque. My neck graft was at least the third for this violin.)

The term BAROQUE VIOLA is very non-specific, referring to any viola of the period in original condition. Violas came in all shapes and sizes. (The very large violas were actually tenors, tuned perhaps an octave below the violin or a fifth below the alto viola.)

The BAROQUE CELLO too was not standardized, but like the baroque violin and viola, it had the short fingerboard, the neck attached flush to the upper ribs with nails through the block, and the characteristic bridge, tailpiece, etc.

VIOLA D'AMORE

Of the European bowed instruments with sympathetic strings, only the viola d'amore sees significant modern use (if we except the Norwegian Hardanger fiddle). It is unfretted with flame-shaped sound holes and (typically) a carved head, held like, and about the same body length as, the modern viola. It has (usually) seven stopped strings and seven metal sympathetic strings.

The stopped (and bowed) strings are typically tuned in D major (A2, D3, A3, D4, F#4, A4, D5), or otherwise depending on the key of the composition and the playing technique. The sympathetic strings are usually tuned in unison with the respective stopped strings.
(The viola d'amore is epitomized in the fine work of Johann Ulrich Eberle; my mother's name was Eberle, and I like to think of him as a possible relative.)

A related instrument, the baryton, a sort of bass viol with many sympathetic strings, is rare.

THE VIOL FAMILY

In the 1500's the viols and the violin family were already distinct. The violin family had essentially superseded the viols by 1700. The viols have undergone a modest 20th century revival.

These usually had six (occasionally 5 or 7) thin gut strings, seven tied frets, flat backs, sloping shoulders, C-shaped sound holes, carved heads, and flush edges. An end pin was not used.

Most were tuned in fourths, with a third between the two middle strings. They used outcurved bows held underhand.

Our present double bass violin was developed from the double bass viol.

The more important of the viols are listed here with their typical body lengths and tuning. The numeric suffixes indicate octave numbers as above.

VIOL NAME	NOMINAL BODY LENGTH	TUNING, STRINGS 6 TO 1
TREBLE	370 mm	D3 G3 C4 E4 A4 D5
TENOR	500 mm	A fifth below the TREBLE
BASS ("GAMBA")	700 mm	An octave below the TREBLE
DOUBLE BASS	1020 mm	An octave below the BASS

HISTORICAL NOTE

Historical instruments tend to be vague in terminology with many variations in design and tuning. Further elaboration or a special bibliography (which could be voluminous) are outside our present scope. Nor is this an area of special interest or expertise for me. But see "Shapes of the Baroque" in the bibliography. Here is a list of only some of the principal names by language.

ENGLISH	FRENCH	GERMAN	ITALIAN
violin	violon	Geige	violino
viola	alto	Bratsche	viola (da braccio)
cello	violoncelle	Cello	violoncello
double bass	contrebasse	Kontrabass	contrabbasso
viola d'amore	viole d'amour	Liebesgeige	viola d'amore
treble viol	dessus de viole	diskant Gambe	viola da gamba (soprano)
tenor viol	tenor de viole	tenor Gambe	viola da gamba (tenore)
bass viol	basse de viole	bass Gambe	viola da gamba (basso)
double bass viol	contrebasse de viole	kontrabass Gambe	violone

Anyone building "early" instruments will work from authentic examples or museum data. These instruments are so varied that reliable adjustment data cannot be given here. As an item of possible interest, I have, however, tabulated below some old adjustment data from Tolbecque.

SOME ADJUSTMENT DATA AFTER L'ART DU LUTHIER, 1903	ALTO VIOLA	TENOR VIOLA	VIOLA D'AMORE	BASS VIOL
Spacing of Outside Strings at Nut	18	20	34	36
Spacing of Outside Strings at Bridge	38	40	68	76
First String Fingerboard Clearance	4.5	5.0	4.5	4.0
Last String Fingerboard Clearance	5.5	6.0	5.5	6.0
Bridge Thickness at Strings	2.0	2.5	2.5	3.0
Bridge Thickness at Feet	5.0	7.0	6.0	14
Fingerboard Radius of Curvature			72	76

NEW VIOLIN "OCTET"

Over the past 30 years the Catgut Acoustical Society has proposed and developed a "new violin family" based on certain acoustic considerations, covering a wide range, with consistent placement of the air resonances. These instruments have not been widely accepted, but they are being made and played. See the table on the next page.

NEW VIOLIN FAMILY NAME	BODY LENGTH	RIB HEIGHT	TUNING RELATIVE TO THE TRADITIONAL VIOLIN FAMILY
TREBLE	286	20	An Octave above the Violin
SOPRANO	312	20	An octave above the Viola
MEZZO	382	25	Same as the Violin
ALTO	508	30	Same as the Viola
TENOR	654	40	An Octave below the Violin
BARITONE	864	50	Same as the Cello
SMALL BASS	1042	180	A Fourth above the Double Bass
CONTRABASS	1300	240	Same as the Double Bass

MISCELLANEOUS OTHERS

To many people, the word FIDDLE means the violin as used in folk or "country" music. It is played mostly in the first position, sometimes with consummate skill. Scordatura or "cross tuning" is often used to facilitate special effects or playing in different keys. Steel strings and a flatter bridge are the usual departures from standard adjustment. The violin maker will work on these (and perhaps electric versions, too), but they are outside the scope of this book.

The unusual MUTE VIOLIN is for quiet practice; the body is largely cut away. (I recently restored one by Gand & Bernardel.)

The POCHETTE, pocket violin or kit, was made in various bizarre shapes.

The 19th century German BOWED ZITHER is tuned like the violin; it is fretted and placed on a table in front of the player. (I have one as a wall decoration.)

There are many other bowed folk instruments, ranging from the hurdy-gurdy, with an integral rotary bow, to the odd and obsolete trumpet marine, but they remain outside our interest here.

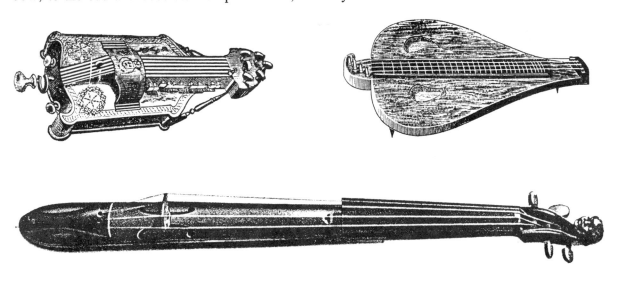

HE TOOK IT UP, GAVE IT ONE TWIRL ROUND AND SATISFIED HIMSELF IT WAS A FIDDLE.

Jack of All Trades, Chapter I.

An engraving from the 19th century novel by Charles Reade (Peter Fenelon Collier edition) based on the life of the English violin maker John Lott. Here Thomas Dodd checks the adjustment of the apprentice Lott's sample violin.

CHAPTER 5

FURTHER REFERENCE

INTRODUCTION

These are the books that seem most relevant to our subject. There are doubtless others that I have not studied or may not be aware of. There are lots of good fiddle books that are excluded here, concerned as they are more with history, makers, collecting, dealing, and esthetics.

BIBLIOGRAPHY

Arakelian, Sourene: PRECEPTS AND OBSERVATIONS OF A LUTHIER, Verlag Das Musikinstrument, Frankfurt, 1987. Worthwhile views on violin making, graduation, and adjustment.

Bolander, John Alfred: VIOLIN BOW MAKING, Boyd Poulsen, San Mateo, California, 1981. One of the few good books on the subject.

Burgan, Arthur: BASIC STRING REPAIRS, Oxford University Press, London 1974. For the teacher or player.

Elgar, Raymond : INTRODUCTION TO THE DOUBLE BASS, The author, Sussex, 1960. General, with a useful section on making. His MORE ABOUT THE DOUBLE BASS, 1963, includes a section on repair.

Ford, Charles (Editor): MAKING MUSICAL INSTRUMENTS, Pantheon, NY, 1977. Includes Dietrich Kessler on making a bass viol, Adam Paul on making a violin (including baroque), and Friedemann Hellwig on restoration and conservation of historical instruments. A brief overview.

Geiger, Leroy & Cole, L. M.: VIOLIN MAKING MADE CLEAR AND CONCISE, LaFosse Music House, Chicago 1935. Exactly what the title says. The late Leon LaFosse, a Mittenwald graduate, was my first guide in violin making when I was an engineer in Palo Alto, California in the 1960's.

Gruppo Studi Liutari (under Gio Batta Morassi): THE VIOLIN AND ITS REDUCED SIZES, Cremona 1980. Includes full size outlines of different models.

Henderson, Frank V.: HOW TO MAKE A VIOLIN BOW, Murray, Seattle, 1977. Another good book on the subject.

Heron-Allen, Ed.: VIOLIN-MAKING, AS IT WAS AND IS, Ward Lock & Co., Ltd., London, 1885. Antiquated, encyclopedic, this English classic is still worthwhile background reading for violin makers. Available in reprint.

Hill, W. Henry, Arthur F., and Alfred E.: ANTONIO STRADIVARI, HIS LIFE AND WORK, London, 1902, Dover reprint, New York, 1963. Reliable descriptions and measurements of original instruments.

Lamb, Norman: A GUIDE TO TEACHING STRINGS, Wm. C. Brown Co., Dubuque, Iowa, 1971. Includes MENC requirements and general information on instruments.

Leonhardt, Konrad: GEIGENBAU UND KLANGFRAGE, Verlag Das Musikinstrument, Frankfurt am Main 1969. The author was Director of the Mittenwald Geigenbauschule. Acoustical experiments, the translucency graduation method, and dimensions.

Metropolitan Music: PROFESSIONAL HINTS ON REPAIR, Stowe, Vermont, n.d. A booklet containing bow and instrument sizes and adjustment suggestions.

Millant, Max et Roger: MANUEL PRACTIQUE DE LUTHERIE, Larousse, Paris 1952. A classic handbook on making and repair. Recommended.

Möckel, Otto and Winckel, Fritz: DIE KUNST DES GEIGENBAUES, Verlag Handwerk und Technik, Hamburg 1977. Moeckel's practical classic of 1930 on making and repair updated by Winckel. Recommended.

Monical, William L.: SHAPES OF THE BAROQUE, American Federation of Violin and Bow Makers, Inc., William L. Monical, Staten Island, NY, 1989. Catalog of the exhibition of unaltered baroque instruments at Lincoln Center in New York.

Nicolini, Gualtiero, e Scolari, Giorgio: COME NASCE UN VIOLINO (THE BIRTH OF A VIOLIN), Ed. Stradivari, Cremona, 1985. Straightforward, well illustrated description of the classical process with a partial English translation.

Peterlongo, Paolo: THE VIOLIN, Paul Elek, London, 1973. Simplified acoustical discussion and more general violin topics.

Petherick, Horace: THE REPAIRING AND RESTORATION OF VIOLINS, The Strad Library, London, 1903. An unusual book exclusively on this subject. 200 readable pages on turn of the century repair techniques, largely still applicable.

Pickering, Norman C.: THE BOWED STRING, Amereon, NY, 1991. Available from the author, 23 Culver Hill, Southampton NY. *The* book on strings. Authoritative and enlightening.

Reid, Joseph V.: YOU CAN MAKE A STRADIVARIUS VIOLIN, Popular Mechanics Press, Chicago 1958. Excellent set of drawings.

Robertson, William K.: FIDDLEMAKER'S WORKSHEETS, Argus Books, Hemel Hempstead, UK, 1983. An English method, clear drawings.

Rödig, Hans Joh.: DER NEUE WEG, NATURWISSENSCHAFTEN IM GEIGENBAU, Verlag Das Musikinstrument, Frankfurt, 1974. Interesting rationale of static forces and their effect on tone production.

Roussel, Andre': GRUNDLAGEN DER GEIGE UND DES GEIGENBAUES, Verlag Das Musikinstrument, Frankfurt am Main 1973. Theories and methods of adjustment. Translated into German by Adolph Koenig, Director of the Brienz, Switzerland Geigenbauschule.

Sacconi, Simone F.: THE "SECRETS" OF STRADIVARI, Libreria del Convegno, Cremona 1979. The modern violin maker's Bible. Essential.

St. George, Henry: FIDDLES: THEIR SELECTION, PRESERVATION, AND BETTERMENT, The Strad Library, London, 1910. A pleasant and sound little book.

Tolbecque, A.: L'ART DU LUTHIER, Th. Mercier, Niort, 1903. Comprehensive if somewhat dated. Detailed on repair. Reprint, Broude, New York, 1969.

Wake, H.S.: THE TECHNIQUE OF VIOLIN MAKING, The author, San Diego, California, 1973. A popular, practical "how to" book.

Weisshaar, Hans, and Shipman, Margaret: VIOLIN RESTORATION, A MANUAL FOR VIOLIN MAKERS, The authors, Los Angeles, 1989. Comprehensive and well illustrated, unique in this field.

PERIODICALS

The newsletters, magazines, and journals listed below frequently carry useful articles. They are also a way of keeping in touch with suppliers, colleagues, customers, etc.

AMERICAN LUTHERIE. Quarterly Journal of the Guild of American Luthiers. For the guitar maker but includes excellent violin articles. GAL C/O Tim Olsen, 8222 South Park Ave, Tacoma WA 98408 USA

The BULLETIN of the SOUTHERN CALIFORNIA ASSOCIATION OF VIOLIN MAKERS. Monthly. SCAVM C/O Leonard C. Showalter, 2249 Cardinal Drive, San Diego CA 92123 USA

The JOURNAL OF THE CATGUT ACOUSTICAL SOCIETY. Semi-annual. Research papers and sometimes practical conclusions and methods. CAS C/O Carleen Hutchins, 112 Essex Avenue, Montclair NJ 07042 USA

The JOURNAL of the VIOLIN MAKERS ASSOCIATION OF ARIZONA, INTERNATIONAL. Monthly. VMAAI C/O Bill Scruggs, 1137 Los Serenos, Fillmore CA 93015 USA

The JOURNAL OF THE VIOLIN SOCIETY OF AMERICA. An elegant professional quarterly. VSA C/O Ed Campbell, 814 Lerew Road, Boiling Springs PA 17007 USA

MICHIGAN VIOLINMAKERS ASSOCIATION NEWSLETTER. Quarterly. MVA C/O David Brownell, 2187 Yorktown, Ann Arbor MI 48105 USA

NOTE: The periodicals above are provided to members in the respective associations.

THE STRAD. Monthly magazine for players and makers. Fine color photographs and studies of classic instruments. Orpheus Publications Ltd., PO Box 648, Harrow, Middlesex HA1 2NW

STRINGS. Magazine for players and makers. Six issues a year. Strings, PO Box 767, San Anselmo CA 94960 USA

NOTE: The mailing addresses above were current at the time of this printing, April, 1995.

"TERM TRANSLATOR"

For those who read French, German, or Italian more or less haltingly, as I do, there follows a short cross reference of about 200 violin and bow related terms. (See also page 28 for the principal instrument names.) Actually, the first section, English to French, German, and Italian, may serve as a partial glossary for international readers of this book, while the subsequent sections, French, German, and Italian to English, may be helpful to those reading books or catalogs in those languages. Such a short list, including few synonyms, is necessarily quite limited, given the richness of language, much as a list of single-valued measurements is limited, given the variety in instruments. For example, "on the quarter" in Italian may be "di quarto, assiale, radiale, a cuneo, a spicchio", etc. Simple, root words were preferred to compound words such as Adergrabenschneider (Purfling-groove-cutter). Among other complications is the difference in diminutives, e.g. seghetto for small saw (sega). I have omitted some of the quaint anatomical designations, which seem to defy standardization. For example, the "toes, feet, legs, knees/noses, eyes/kidneys, ears, and heart, etc." of the bridge and the "chin, throat, etc." of the scroll. My selection has been largely arbitrary, based on limited reading, nor does every word have an exact correspondent in the other languages. Not being fluent in these languages, I hope the reader will be tolerant of any lapses.

ENGLISH TO:	FRENCH	GERMAN	ITALIAN
adjustment	réglage	Regulierung	regolamento
alizarin/madder	alizari/garance	Alizarin/Krapp	alizarina/robbia
angle	angle	Winkel	angolo
arching	voûte	Wölbung	bombatura
arching guides	modèles de voûte	Wölbungskurven	quinte
back	fond	Boden	fondo
backplate, frog	talon	Zwickel	ginocchio
balsam	baume	Balsam	balsamo
bass bar	barre	Bassbalken	catena
belly/top	table	Decke	piano armonico
bending iron	fer à plier	Biegeeisen	ferro piega-fasce
black	noir	Schwartz	nero
block	tasseau	Klotz	zocchetto/tassello
blue	bleu	blau	blu
body	corps	Corpus	cassa armonica
bow	archet	Bogen	arco
bowed	instrument à cordes	Streichinstrument	strumento ad
boxwood	buis	Buchsbaum	bosso
breast patch	pièce d'estomac	Brustfutter	fodera centrale
bridge	chevalet	Steg	ponticello
brown	brun	braun	bruno
brush	pinceau	Pinsel	pennello
bushing, pegs	bouchage	ausbüchsen	rifari i buchi
button, back	talon	Bodenplattchen	nocetta
button, bow	bouton	Schraubenknopf	bottone
c-bout	c	C-bogen	c
caliper, grad.	compas d'épaisseur	Stärkenzirkel	spessimetro
camber	cambrure	Krümmung	curvatura
case	étui	Etui	cassa
chamfer	chanfrein	Kante	nastrino
channel	gorge	Hohlkehle	sguisciatura
cheeks, pegbox	joues	Wange	ganasce
chin rest	mentonnière	Kinnhalter	mentoniera
chisel	ciseau	Flachbeitel	scalpello
clamp	happe	Klammer	morsetta
clearance, string	hauteur	Zwischenraum	altezza
cleats	tacquets	RissklÖtchen	piastrine
coat, varnish	couche	Schicht	mano
coloring	couleurs	Farbstoffe	coloranti
copal	copal	Kopal	coppale
corner	coin	Ecke	punta
crack	cassure	Riss	crepa
diameter	diamètre	Durchmesser	diametro
dividers	compas	Stechzirkel	compasso
dragon's blood	sangdragon	Drachenblut	sangue di drago
drill	chignole	Bohrer	trapano
ear/eye, scroll	bouton	Ohr	perno centrale
ebony	ebene	Ebenholz	ebano
edge	bord	Rand	bordo
end button	bouton	Knopf	bottone
end pin	pique	Stachel	puntone
eye/ear, scroll	bouton	Ohr	perno centrale
eyelet	écrou	Schraubenmutter	madrevite
f-holes	ouïes/ff	f-LÖcher	fori
feet, bridge	pieds	füsse	piedini
ferrule	passant	Ring	anello
file	lime	Feile	lima
fingerbd.	renversement	Griffbrettlage	positione..tastier
fingerboard	touche	Griffbrett	tastiera
fitting up	montage	montieren	montatura
flamed	ondé	geflammt	marezzato/fiamm
fluting	coulisse	Hohlkehle	scannelatura
frog, bow	hausse	Frosch	tallone
gamboge	gomme-gutte	Gummigutti	gomma gutta
glue	colle	Leim	colla
gold	or	Gold	oro
gouge	gouge	Hohlbeitel	sgorbia
graduation	faire les épaisseurs	Ausarbeitung	fare i spessori
graft, neck	enture	Anschäfter	innesto
green	vert	grün	verde
grip, bow	poucette	Daumenleder	fascia in cuoio
groove, purfling	mortaise	Graben	canale
ground	encollage	Grundierung	preparazione
gum	gomme	Harz	resina
gut	boyau	Darm	budello
hair	crins	Haare	crini
head, bow	tête	Kopf	nasetto
head, instrument	tête	Schnecke	testa
heel, neck	pied	Halsfuss	piede
height	hauteur	Höhe	altezza
hollowing out	creusage	Ausholung	scavatura
hurdy-gurdy	vielle à roue	Leierkasten	ghironda
in the white	en blanc	im Weiss	in bianco
ivory	ivoire	Elfenbein	avorio
joint	joint	Fuge	giunta
kit	pochette	Taschengeige	pochette
knife	canif	Schnitzmesser	coltello
label	étiquette	Zettel/Etikett	etichetta
length	longeur	Länge	lunghezza
lining	contra-éclisse	Reifchen	controfascia
linseed oil	huile de lin	Leinöl	olio di lino
lower	inférieur	Unter	inferiore
madder/alizarin	garance/alizari	Krapp/Alizarin	robbia/alizarina
maple	érable	Ahorn	acero
mastic	mastic	Mastix	mastice
measurements	mesure	Messungen	misure
middle	moyen	Mittel	centrale
mirror, sound	miroir	Stimmspiegel	specchio
mold	moule	Form	sagoma/forma
mute	sourdine	Dämpfer	sordino
neck	poignée/manche	Hals	manico
notches, f-holes	crans	Kerben	tacche/taglietti
nut, fingerboard	sillet du haut	Obersattel	capotasto
oil	huile	Öl	olio
on the quarter	sur sens	nach dem Spiegel	di quarto/radiale
on the slab	sur couche	nachder Schwarte	di
orange	orange	orange	arancio
outline	contour	Umriss	contorno
parchment	parchemin	Pergament	pergamena
patch	pièce/doublure	Futter	fodera
pattern/template	modèle	Schablone/Modell	modello
pear wood	poirier	Birnbaum	pero
pearl	nacre	Perlmutter	madreperla
peg	cheville	Wirbel	pirolo/bischero
peg shaper	taille-chevilles	Wirbelfräser	temperino
pegbox	chevillier	Wirbelkasten	scatola dei piroli
pernambuco	fernambouc	Pernambuk	pernambuco
pins, gluing	goupilles	Stifte	chiodini
plane, large	varlope	Rauhbank	piallo
plane, small	rabot	Hobel	pialletta
plaster cast	contrepartie	Formzulage, Gips	controsagoma
plywood	contreplaque	Sperrholz	multistrato
poplar	peuplier	Pappel	pioppo
propolis	propolis	Bienenkittharz	propoli
pumice	ponce	Bimsstein	pomice
purfling	filetage	Einlage/Adern	filettatura
purfling cutter	tracoir à filets	Adergrabenschnei	filettatore
radius	rayon	Halbmesser \der	raggio
reamer	alésoir	Wirbelbohrer	alesatore
red	rouge	rot	rosso
rehair	remêcher	behaaren	incrinare
repair	reparation	Reparatur	riparazione
restoration	restauration	Wiederherstellung	restauro
rib	éclisse	Zarge	fascia
rosewood	palissandre	Palisander	palissandro
rosin	colophane	Kolophonium	resina
roughing out	ébouchage	ausstossen	sgrossatura
saddle	sillet du bas	Untersattel	tasto inferiore
sandarac	sandaraque	Sandarack	sandracca
saw	scie	Säge	sega
scraper	ratissoir	Zieheklinge	rasiera
screw	vis	Schraube	vite
scroll	coquille	Schnecke	riccio/chiocchiol
setting the neck	enclavement	Halsansatz	incastro
shellac	gomme laque	Körnerlack	gommalacca
silver wire	fil d'argent	Silberdraht	filo d'argento
size	grosseur	Grüsse	grandezza
slide	recouvrement	Schub	slitta
sound post	âme	Stimme	anima
sound post crack	cassure d'âme	Stimmriss	crepa
sound post patch	piece d'âme	Stimmfutter	fodera sopra
sound post setter	pointe a âme	Stimmsetzer	ferro del'anima
spacing, string	ecartment	Entfernung	distanza
spirit	alcool	Spiritus	spirito
spruce	sapin	Fichte	abete
stain	teint	beize	tinta
stick	baguette	Stange	bacchetta
stop, body	diapason	Mensur	diapason
string	corde	Saite	corda
tailpiece	cordier	Saitenhalter	cordiera
tailpice fastener	corde d'attache	Haltersaite	staffa
tap tone	son frappé	Klopfton	suono bassato
template/pattern	modèle	Modell/Schablone	modello
thickness	épaissur	Stärke	spessore
tip, bow	plaque de tête	Kopfplatte	piastrina di
tone color	timbre	Klangfarbe	timbro
tool	outil	Werkzeug	attrezzo
top/belly	table	Deck	tavola armonica
tortoise shell	écaille	Schildpatt	tartaruga
trumpet marine	trompette marine	Trumscheit	tromba marina
tuning	accord	Stimmung	accordatura
tuning fork	diapason	Stimmgabel	diapason
turpentine	térebenthine	Terpentinöl	trementina
underslide, frog	coulisse	Bahn	piastrina
upper	supérieur	Ober	superiore
varnish	vernis	Lack	vernice
violin maker	luthier	Geigenbauer	liutaio
volute, scroll	volute	Windung	spirale
wedge	cale	Keil	cuneo
whalebone	fanon de baleine	Fischbein	stecca di balena
width	largeur	Breite	larghezza
willow	saule	Weide	salice
wing	bique	Flügel/Lappen	paletta
wolf tone	loup	Wolfston	lupo
wood	bois	Holz	legno
worm holes	ravage des vers	wurmstichig	tarlato
wrapping	garniture	Bewicklung	avvolgimento
yellow	jaune	gelb	giallo

FRENCH TO:	ENGLISH	FRENCH TO:	ENGLISH	FRENCH TO:	ENGLISH	FRENCH TO:	ENGLISH
accord	tuning	corps	body	inférieur	lower	propolis	propolis
alcool	spirit	couche	coat, varnish	instrument à cordes	bowed	rabot	plane, small
alésoir	reamer	couleurs	coloring	ivoire	ivory	ratissoir	scraper
alizari/garance	alizarin/madder	coulisse	fluting	jaune	yellow	ravage des vers	worm holes
âme	sound post	coulisse	underslide, frog	joint	joint	rayon	radius
angle	angle	crans	notches, f-holes	joues	cheeks, pegbox	recouvrement	slide
appui/saille	fb. ht. over edge	creusage	hollowing out	largeur	width	réglage	adjustment
archet	bow	crins	hair	lime	file	remêcher	rehair
baguette	stick	diamètre	diameter	longeur	length	renversement	fingerbd.
barre	bass bar	diapason	stop, body	loup	wolf tone	reparation	repair
baume	balsam	diapason	tuning fork	luthier	violin maker	restauration	restoration
bique	wing	ebene	ebony	mastic	mastic	rouge	red
bleu	blue	ébouchage	roughing out	mentonnière	chin rest	sandaraque	sandarac
bois	wood	écaille	tortoise shell	mesure	measurements	sangdragon	dragon's blood
bord	edge	ecartment	spacing, string	miroir	mirror,	sapin	spruce
bouchage	bushing, pegs	éclisse	rib	modèle	pattern/template	saule	willow
bouton	ear/eye, scroll	écrou	eyelet	modèle	template/pattern	scie	saw
bouton	button, bow	en blanc	in the white	modèles de voûte	arching guides	sillet du haut	nut, fingerboard
bouton	end button	enclavement	setting the neck	montage	fittings	sillet du bas	saddle
boyau	gut	encollage	ground	mortaise	groove, purfling	son frappé	tap tone
brun	brown	enture	graft, neck	moule	mold	sourdine	mute
buis	boxwood	épaissur	thickness	moyen	middle	supérieur	upper
cale	wedge	érable	maple	nacre	pearl	sur couche	on the slab
cambrure	camber	étiquette	label	noir	black	sur sens	on the quarter
canif	knife	étui	case	ondé	flamed	table	top/belly
cassure d'âme	sound post crack	faire les épaisseurs	graduation	or	gold	tacquets	cleats
cassure	crack	fanon de baleine	whalebone	orange	orange	taille-chevilles	peg shaper
chanfrein	chamfer	fer à plier	bending iron	ouïes/ff	f-holes	talon	backplate, frog
chevalet	bridge	fernambouc	pernambuco	outil	tool	talon	button, back
cheville	peg	fil d'argent	silver wire	palissandre	rosewood	tasseau	block
chevillier	pegbox	filetage	purfling	parchemin	parchment	teint	stain
chignole	drill	fond	back	passant	ferrule	térebenthine	turpentine
ciseau	chisel	garance/alizari	madder/alizarin	peuplier	poplar	tête	head, bow
coin	corner	garniture	wrapping	pièce d'âme	sound post patch	tête	head, instrument
colle	glue	gomme	gum	pièce/doublure	patch	timbre	tone color
colophane	rosin	gomme laque	shellac	pièce d'estomac	breast patch	touche	fingerboard
compas d'épaisseur	caliper, grad.	gomme-gutte	gamboge	pied	heel, neck	tracoir à filets	purfling cutter
compas	dividers	gorge	channel	pieds	feet, bridge	trompette marine	trumpet marine
contour	outline	gouge	gouge	pinceau	brush	varlope	plane, large
contra-éclisse	lining	goupilles	pins, guide	pique	end pin	vernis	varnish
contrepartie	plaster cast	grosseur	size	plaque de tête	tip, bow	vert	green
contreplaque	plywood	happe	clamp	pochette	kit	vielle à roue	hurdy-gurdy
copal	copal	hausse	frog, bow	poignée/manche	neck	vis	screw
coquille	scroll	hauteur	height	pointe a âme	sound post setter	volute	volute, scroll
corde d'attache	tailpiece fastener	hauteur	clearance, string	poirier	pear wood	voûte	arching
corde	string	huile di lin	linseed oil	ponce	pumice		
cordier	tailpiece	huile	oil	poucette	grip, bow		

GERMAN TO:	ENGLISH	GERMAN TO:	ENGLISH	GERMAN TO:	ENGLISH	GERMAN TO:	ENGLISH
Adergrabenschnei-	purfling cutter	Flachbeitel	chisel	Krapp/Alizarin	madder/alizarin	Schraubenmutter	eyelet
Ahorn \der	maple	Flügel/Lappen	wing	Krümmung	camber	Schub	slide
Alizarin/Krapp	alizarin/madder	Form	mold	Lack	varnish	Schulterkisse	shoulder pad
Anschäfter	graft, neck	Formzulage, Gips	plaster cast	Länge	length	Schwartz	black
Ausarbeitung	graduation	Frosch	frog, bow	Leierkasten	hurdy-gurdy	Silberdraht	silver wire
ausbüchsen	bushing, pegs	Fuge	joint	Leim	glue	Sperrholz	plywood
Ausholung	hollowing out	füsse	feet, bridge	Leinöl	linseed oil	Spiritus	spirit
ausstossen	roughing out	Futter	patch	Mastix	mastic	Stachel	end pin
Bahn	underslide, frog	Garnitur	fittings	Mensur	stop, body	Stange	stick
Balsam	balsam	geflammt	flamed	Messungen	measurements	Stärke	thickness
Bassbalken	bass bar	Geigenbauer	violin maker	Mittel	middle	Stärkenzirkel	caliper, grad.
behaaren	rehair	gelb	yellow	Modell/Schablone	template/pattern	Stechzirkel	dividers
beize	stain	Gold	gold	montieren	fitting up	Steg	bridge
Bewicklung	wrapping	Graben	groove, purfling	nach dem Spiegel	on the quarter	Stifte	pins, gluing guide
Biegeeisen	bending iron	Griffbrett	fingerboard	nach der Schwarte	on the slab	Stimme	sound post
Bienenkittharz	propolis	Griffbrettlage	fingerbd. project.	Neusilber	German silver	Stimmfutter	sound post patch
Bimsstein	pumice	grün	green	Ober	upper	Stimmgabel	tuning fork
Birnbaum	pear wood	Grundierung	ground	Obersattel	nut, fingerboard	Stimmriss	sound post crack
blau	blue	Grüsse	size	Ohr	eye/ear, scroll	Stimmsetzer	sound post setter
Boden	back	Gummigutti	gamboge	Öl	oil	Stimmspiegel	mirror, sound
Bodenplattchen	button, back	Haare	hair	orange	orange	Stimmung	tuning
Bogen	bow	Halbmesser	radius	Palisander	rosewood	Streichinstrument	bowed instrument
Bohrer	drill	Hals	neck	Pappel	poplar	Taschengeige	kit
braun	brown	Halsansatz	setting the neck	Pergament	parchment	Terpentinöl	turpentine
Breite	width	Halsfuss	heel, neck	Perlmutter	pearl	Trumscheit	trumpet marine
Brustfutter	breast patch	Haltersaite	tailpice fastener	Pernambuk	pernambuco	Umriss	outline
Buchsbaum	boxwood	Harz	gum	Pinsel	brush	Unter	lower
C-bogen	c-bout	Hobel	plane, small	Rand	edge	Untersattel	saddle
Corpus	body	Höhe	height	Rauhbank	plane, large	Vorstand	fb. ht. over edge
Dämpfer	mute	Hohlbeitel	gouge	Regulierung	adjustment	Wange	cheeks, pegbox
Darm	gut	Hohlkehle	fluting/channel	Reifchen	lining	Weide	willow
Daumenleder	grip, bow	Holz	wood	Reparatur	repair	Werkzeug	tool
Decke	belly/top	im Weiss	in the white	Ring	ferrule	Wiederherstellung	restoration
Drachenblut	dragon's blood	Kante	chamfer	Riss	crack	Windung	volute, scroll
Durchmesser	diameter	Karnies	cornice	Rissklötchen	cleats	Winkel	angle
Ebenholz	ebony	Keil	wedge	rot	red	Wirbel	peg
Ecke	corner	Kerben	notches, f-holes	Säge	saw	Wirbelbohrer	reamer
Edelstahl	stainless steel	Kinnhalter	chin rest	Saite	string	Wirbelfräser	peg shaper
Einlage/Adern	purfling	Klammer	clamp	Saitenhalter	tailpiece	Wirbelkasten	pegbox
Elfenbein	ivory	Klangfarbe	tone color	Sandarack	sandarac	Wölbung	arching
Entfernung	spacing, string	Klopfton	tap tone	Schablone/Modell	pattern/template	Wölbungskurven	arching guides
Etui	case	Klotz	block	Schicht	coat, varnish	Wolfston	wolf tone
f-LOcher	f-holes	Knopf	end button	Schildpatt	tortoise shell	wurmstichig	worm holes
Farbstoffe	coloring materials	Kolophonium	rosin	Schnecke	scroll	Zarge	rib
Feile	file	Kopal	copal	Schnecke	head, instrument	Zettel/Etikett	label
Feinstimmer	fine tuner	Kopf	head, bow	Schnitzmesser	knife	Zieheklinge	scraper
Fichte	spruce	Kopfplatte	tip, bow	Schraube	screw	Zwickel	backplate, frog
Fischbein	whalebone	Körnerlack	shellac	Schraubenknopf	button, bow	Zwischenraum	clearance, string

ITALIAN TO:	ENGLISH	ITALIAN TO:	ENGLISH	ITALIAN TO:	ENGLISH	ITALIAN TO:	ENGLISH
abete	spruce	di quarto/radiale	on the quarter	misure	measurements	rifari i buchi	bushing, pegs
accordatura	tuning	di scorza/tangenz.	on the slab	modello	pattern/template	riparazione	repair
acero	maple	diametro	diameter	modello	template/pattern	robbia/alizarina	madder/alizarin
alesatore	reamer	diapason	stop, body	montatura	fitting up	rosso	red
alizarina/robbia	alizarin/madder	diapason	tuning fork	morsetto	clamp	sagoma/forma	mold
altezza	height	distanza	spacing, string	multistrato	plywood	salice	willow
altezza	clearance, string	ebano	ebony	nasetto	head, bow	sandracca	sandarac
anello	ferrule	etichetta	label	nastrino	chamfer	sangue di drago	dragon's blood
angolo	angle	fare i spessori	graduation	nero	black	scalpello	chisel
anima	sound post	fascia	rib	nocetta	button, back	scannellatura	fluting
arancio	orange	fascia in cuoio	grip, bow	olio	oil	scatola dei piroli	pegbox
arco	bow	ferro piega-fasce	bending iron	olio di lino	linseed oil	scavatura	hollowing out
attrezzo	tool	ferro del'anima	sound post setter	oro	gold	sega	saw
avorio	ivory	filettatore	purfling cutter	paletta	wing	sgorbia	gouge
avvolgimento	wrapping	filettatura	purfling	palissandro	rosewood	sgrossatura	roughing out
bacchetta	stick	filo d'argento	silver wire	pennello	brush	sgusciatura	channel
balsamo	balsam	fodera	patch	pergamena	parchment	slitta	slide
blu	blue	fodera sopra	sound post patch	pernambuco	pernambuco	sordino	mute
bombatura	arching	fodera centrale	breast patch	perno centrale	eye/ear, scroll	specchio	mirror, soundpost
bordo	edge	fondo	back	perno centrale	ear/eye, scroll	spessimetro	caliper, grad.
bosso	boxwood	fori armonici/effe	f-holes	pero	pear wood	spessore	thickness
bottone	end button	ganasce	cheeks, pegbox	pialletta	plane, small	spirale	volute, scroll
bottone	button, bow	ghironda	hurdy-gurdy	piallo	plane, large	spirito	spirit
bruno	brown	giallo	yellow	piano armonico	belly/top	staffa	tailpiece fastener
budello	gut	ginocchio	backplate, frog	piastrina di avorio	tip, bow	stecca di balena	whalebone
canale	groove, purfling	giunta	joint	piastrina	underslide, frog	strumento ad arco	bowed instrument
capotasto	nut, fingerboard	gomma gutta	gamboge	piastrine	cleats	suono bassato	tap tone
cassa	case	gommalacca	shellac	piede	heel, neck	superiore	upper
cassa armonica	body	grandezza	size	piedini	feet, bridge	tacche/taglietti	notches, f-holes
catena	bass bar	in bianco	in the white	pioppo	poplar	tallone	frog, bow
centrale	middle	incastro	setting the neck	pirolo/bischero	peg	tarlato	worm holes
chiodini	pins, guide	incrinare	rehair	pochette	kit	tartaruga	tortoise shell
colla	glue	inferiore	lower	pomice	pumice	tastiera	fingerboard
coloranti	coloring materials	innesto	graft, neck	ponticello	bridge	tasto inferiore	saddle
coltello	knife	larghezza	width	positione..tastiera	fingerbd. project.	tavola armonica	top/belly
compasso	dividers	legno	wood	preparazione	ground	temperino	peg shaper
contorno	outline	lima	file	propoli	propolis	testa	head, instrument
controfascia	lining	liutaio	violin maker	punta	corner	timbro	tone color
controsagoma	plaster cast	lunghezza	length	puntone	end pin	tinta	stain
coppale	copal	lupo	wolf tone	quinte	arching guides	trapano	drill
corda	string	madreperla	pearl	raggio	radius	trementina	turpentine
cordiera	tailpiece	madrevite	eyelet	rasiera	scraper	tromba marina	trumpet marine
crepa sopra	sound post crack	manico	neck	regolamento	adjustment	verde	green
crepa	crack	mano	coat, varnish	resina	rosin	vernice	varnish
crini	hair	marezzato/fiamma	flamed	resina	gum	vite	screw
cuneo	wedge	mastice	mastic	restauro	restoration	zocchetto/tassello	block
curvatura	camber	mentoniera	chin rest	riccio/chiocchiolo	scroll		

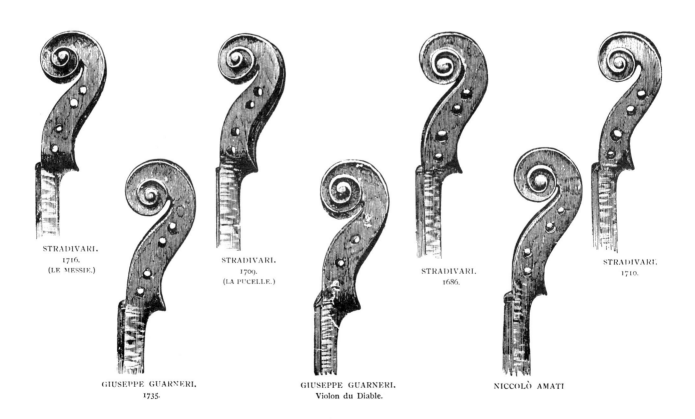

STRADIVARI.
1716.
(LE MESSIE.)

STRADIVARI.
1709.
(LA PUCELLE.)

STRADIVARI.
1686.

STRADIVARI.
1710.

GIUSEPPE GUARNERI.
1735.

GIUSEPPE GUARNERI.
Violon du Diable.

NICCOLÒ AMATI

VIOLINIST'S "NOTES"

The ultimate "measurement" of the violin is in playing it. The violinist thereby identifies its deficiencies, and the skilled violin maker determines whether and how these may best be corrected (neglecting any difficulties in communication).

The evaluation piece reproduced here may be of interest to the violinist, whether or not he is a maker. It is from St. George's book in the Bibliography.

The violinist should check for many qualities, among them the timbre of the sound, "tubby" or "brassy", whether the violin can stand "digging in" or quickly "bottoms out", its pleasantness and purity in double stops, its agility and its responsiveness, noting whether certain spots are dull or ring nicely after the bow leaves the string, and whether the wolf is in evidence.

Violin tone tests should be brief and comparative, the same passage under the same conditions. Carrying power can only be tested comparatively and by a listener.

During tests, it is essential for the player to try to distinguish tone problems from playability ones. For the former an acoustic adjustment, e.g. to the sound post, may be needed, for the latter a mechanical one, e.g. of string clearance or bridge curvature. Of course, sometimes tone and playability problems have a common cause. Every violin has virtues and vices; the violinist determines its net worth.

CHAPTER 6

MAKER'S ADDENDUM

INTRODUCTION

The Table of Additional Measurements on pages 40 and 41 was compiled from and for use in my shop. It includes only the models that I currently make, and will therefore be of less general interest than the foregoing. It is more from the maker's viewpoint and in greater detail. It includes references to my patterns and molds. These are matters of personal artistic preference and are not reproduced here. All dimensions are finished, straight line; measurements taken over the arching using a tape will be greater.

The reader may decide to use the format of this table to record his own model preferences, which will likely differ from mine.
My violin is a more highly arched, narrower, model with an even, singing tone. My viola is a 15 5/8 in "Brescian" style that does not look or sound small, has a full low register and easy response, and requires little adaptation by the violinist. I have made wider, flatter, violins and large violas, but these are my favorites. I like an elegant, interleaved double purfling.
My cello model is drawn from many sources. I have used one piece backs of beautiful Oregon maple.

Instruments have many variations in size, style, and voice. The individual variables in making are not independent, but their ensemble determines the result. I have found the measurements in the table following to be successful, even though modified to a degree in each instrument by intuition, inclination, or imponderables.
In some cases where my values differ significantly from the commonly referred to (Sacconi) ones, these are included in parentheses. This is not done in all cases, and it should be noted that the classical makers varied their measurements from instrument to instrument.

The measurements tell only part of the story. The individual patterns, molds, wood, workmanship, carving style, graduation, varnish, adjustment ... and playing ... tell more.

MEASURING TOOLS

Since our subject is measurements, it seemed appropriate to include here a list of basic measuring tools for the violin shop, along with sample uses. I have not included electronic apparatus that may be used in plate tuning, research,   or manufacturing control.

STEEL TAPE, 6 mm X 2 m, in both mm and inches. To measure all major dimensions, straight or over the arching, and to directly convert English and metric.

VERNIER CALIPER. Reads to 0.1 mm. Side by side English and metric scales convert directly. Used for:
Outside Measurement: Pegbox outside width, neck thickness, sound post diameter, bass bar width, etc.
Inside Measurement: Pegbox inside width, peg hole diameter, string clearance, rib height on violin, etc.
Depth Measurement: Pegbox inside depth, fingerboard projection and surface concavity (used with straight edge), bridge height, bass bar height, etc.

GRADUATING CALIPER. As the name implies, for precise and convenient measurement of top, back, and rib thickness.

REINERT CALIPER. To measure top thickness through the f-holes.

MICROMETER. To measure bow parts, string diameter, etc.

THREAD GAUGE. To identify bow screw threads.

METAL RULES. 300, 500, and 1000 mm or 1, 2, and 3 feet. Straight edges to test fingerboard concavity, and general measurement and layout.

SURFACE PLATE. Plane work base to test or insure flatness.

PROTRACTOR GAUGE. To measure string angle and layout neck angle.

PROFILE GAUGE. Instantly copies arching, fingerboard, bar, bridge and other curves.

PARALLEL MARKING GAUGE(S). To mark edge thickness, fit the bar, etc..

SMALL SQUARE. To test and lay out 90 degree angles.

DIVIDERS. To find centers, divide distances, transfer dimensions between rule and work, and to scribe circles. Proportional (double ended) dividers "automatically" divide or rescale.

SOUND POST LENGTH CALIPER. To measure the approximate required sound post length through the f-hole.

SOUND POST POSITION GAUGE. A cut business card will serve. See the drawing on page 23.

FULL SIZE TEMPLATES. String clearance gauges, bridge templates, arching guides, f-hole patterns . . . . whatever. Make from thin wood, metal, or clear plastic.

GRAM SCALE. To weigh bows, varnish components, etc.

BOW HAIR GAUGE. To measure out standard amounts of hair for bows.

INSPECTION LIGHT AND MIRROR. To see inside an instrument.

MAGNIFYING LENS OR VISOR. To see and work with more precision.

GRADUATING DRILL. A wide capacity drill press to produce guide holes at a precise thickness.

MULTI-LEAF ("feeler") GAUGE. For fast, precise set up of the graduating drill, checking string clearance at the nut, etc.

TUNING FORK. Basic standard of pitch.

ELECTRONIC TUNER. A "hands free" model automatically identifies a tone on the chromatic scale and its sharpness or flatness in hundredths (cents) of a semitone. It can be set to other pitches than A440. It enables precise identification of tap tones.

TABLE OF ADDITIONAL MEASUREMENTS

MAKER'S MEASUREMENTS Page 1 of 2			
(Use with the basic table on page 10)	VIOLIN	VIOLA	CELLO
Body Outline	Refer to Patterns and molds.		
Body Length	358 (354)	397 (412)	755 (759)
Body Width, Upper	165	194	344
Body Width, Middle	109	127	230
Body Width, Lower	204	244	438
Upper Edge of Top to Bridge Center	195	212	400 (402)
Neck Length, Upper Edge of Top to Nut	130	141	280
Ratio of These Two Distances	3:2	3:2	10:7
Neck Length, Nut to Lower End of Neck	138	150	293
Neck Height at Lower End	41	50	140
Neck Width at Lower End	32	33	45
Neck Angle at Lower End, Degrees	83.5	83	82
Neck Width at Back Button	21	22 (23)	28 (30)
Button Length	13 (12.5)	16 (13.5)	23
Saddle Length	36	40	60 (55)
Saddle Height	7.5	9.5	12.5
Saddle Width	6.0	8.0	10
Block Size, Upper	50x15(60x14)	50x18(60x15)	100x30(120x22)
Block Size, Lower	50x12(48x14)	50x14(55x15)	120x30(120x22)
Blocks, Corner	See Molds.		
Block Shape	See Patterns.		
Rib Height at Neck	30	37	115 (120)
Rib Height at Lower Block	31.5 (32)	40 (39)	118 (126)
Rib Thickness	1.0	1.1 (1.0)	1.6 (1.3-1.5)
Lining Thickness	2.0	2.2	3.0
Lining Height	6.0 (8.0)	7.0 (8.0)	14 (19)
Bar Width	5.5	6.0	11
Bar Height at Bridge, Approximate	11 *	12	24
(Others place the maximum height at the bar center.)			
Bar Height at Ends, Approximate	2.0	2.5	5.0
Bar Length (7/9 of the Body Length)	278	309	587
(Others measure in 40, 45, and 80, respectively from each end of the top.)			
Scroll and Neck Outline	Refer to pattern.		
Width of Scroll	42	50	66
Width of Chamfer on Scroll	1.7	1.9	2.2
Peg Ends: Cut off flush with pegbox; finish with a 20 mm radius.			
Peg Taper	1:30	1:30	1:23
Pegbox Width, Upper Inside	10	12	16
Pegbox Width, Lower Inside	14	19	28
Pegbox Side Thickness at Opening	5.0	5.5 (6.0)	8.0
Pegbox Side Thickness at Back	7.5	8.5	10.5
Nut Length	23.5	29	46
Nut Width, Underside	6.0	7.0	9.5

* A traditional height; but I may use up to 14 mm to get the wanted tap tone with the sides of the bar planed to a thin tapered cross section for stiffness with less weight.

(Use with the basic table on page 10)	VIOLIN	VIOLA	CELLO
Bridge Blank Width at Feet	41	50	90
Bridge Foot Height	0.9	1.1	2.0
Bridge Foot Length	11	13	24
Bridge Foot Extension Past the Bar	1.0	1.5	3.0
Bridge Leg Width	4.5	5.0	8.5
Bridge Thickness, Just over the Arch	4.0	4.7	8.0
Arching Height, Top	17 (15.5)	20 (18.5)	27 (25.5)
Arching Height, Back	15 (14.5)	18 (16.5)	24 (22.3)
Arching Shape	Templates, Contour Lines, and Eye.		
f-Hole Outline	Refer to Patterns.		
f-Hole Length, Overall	78	96	145 (140)
Distance between Upper Eyes of f-Holes	41	53	90 (92)
Distance between f-Holes at Bridge	75	86	150
Air Tone, Complete Instrument, Approx.	C4	A3	G2
Tap Tone of Top with f-Holes and Bar	F4	C4	C#3
Top Thickness, Upper	2.5	2.7	4.1
Top Thickness, Sound Post and f-Holes	3.0	3.2	4.5
Top Thickness, Elsewhere	2.6	2.8	4.2
Back Thickness, Upper	2.5	2.7	3.8
Back Thickness, Middle	3.4 - 4.5	3.7 - 5.2	5.0 - 7.0
Back Thickness, Lower	2.6	2.8	4.0
Thickness in Channel	2.4	2.5	4.0
Edge Thickness at Corners	4.5 (5.0)	5.0 (5.5)	6.0
Edge Thickness at C's	4.5	5.0	6.0 (5.5)
Edge Thickness Elsewhere	4.0	4.5	5.5 (5.0)
Edge Overhang at Corners	2.0	2.1	2.8
Edge Overhang Elsewhere	3.0	3.2	4.0 (3.5)
Purfling to Edge	3.8	4.0	5.0 (4.5)
Purfling to Edge (If Double)	7.0	8.7	---
Purfling Width	1.2	1.2	1.8 (1.2)
Purfling Groove Depth	2.5	2.5	2.5
Corner Width	6.7 (7.0)	7.3	10 (9.0)

GRADUATION

Good instruments have been made with many systems of graduation or with no apparent system, with different tap tones and intervals (including backs pitched below the top). Different channel characteristics, rib thickness, neck stiffness, varnish, etc. all modify the tone after the instrument is assembled. Tap tones (mode 5) in the table are representative, but depend on the arching, graduation, and wood characteristics. The top without the bar is about a tone lower. The thicknesses given above are slightly thicker than those given by Sacconi for stiff wood. With lighter, more flexible wood it may be advisable to leave the plates and ribs 10% or so thicker than shown.

Sacconi (see the Bibliography) gives the best basis for graduation, modified by wood characteristics and intuition, the upper areas slightly thinner, the back a semitone higher or lower. Following

Sacconi the center of graduation of the back is about 52% of the way up from the bottom. Millant (see the Bibliography) and others place it under the bridge. I like to make the back a very little thicker on the treble side to balance the sound post, the top a very little thinner on the bass side to allow the bar to control the vibrating area. At least that is the rationale. (Please note that I am referring to making instruments, not regraduating those of other makers, which should never be done without a clear and necessary reason.)

The air tone or "Helmholtz" resonance reinforces the lower register. It is lowered somewhat by larger inside volume, smaller f-hole area, less stiff plates and ribs, looser sound post, and vice versa.

VARNISH

An area for the artist. No recipes, but here are some observations.

OIL and SPIRIT varnish are both good. Oil varnish is resin combined with a drying oil (like linseed). Spirit varnish is resin (gums) dissolved in alcohol &/or essential (evaporating) oils. Other things may be added to plasticize, thin, color, accelerate or retard drying, etc.
A dilute spirit varnish GROUND before and after final scraping improves the finish and its apparent depth. Glue is not a good ground and may cause trouble with cleaning and repair.
Swelling the spring wood of the top before varnishing makes the GRAIN more apparent and interesting.
Little, if any, STAIN should be in the wood. Tanning in the sun is preferred.

A fast drying spirit over a slower oil varnish can create a nice CRACKLE effect.

LESS varnish is better than more, within reason.

Don't risk color FADING; use light fast colors with spirit varnish or permanent artist's colors in oil varnish or as a glaze. Color varnish goes over a yellow varnish over the ground.
An AIR BRUSH is convenient for spirit varnish and for retouching large repairs.

Tripoli with water or oil on a felt pad is good for RUBBING the varnish.

FRENCH POLISHING is applying a good spirit varnish with a cloth pad and oil. An overcoat for spirit varnish and for general repairs.

WOOD

Top wood should be light and stiff with low damping, giving a relatively high, clear, ring when struck. The ratios of stiffness and of sound velocity to density are useful figures of merit.

Very deeply curled maple is in effect partially end grain and less stiff, especially when cut as thin as the depth of the curl. Slab cut maple, especially if quilted, is also less stiff than quartered. These considerations affect the selection of wood, its graduation, its strength and suitability for large or small instruments or for the desired tonality.

At first I used only old European spruce and maple, but I now feel that the wood here in Oregon, if carefully selected and seasoned, is second to none. I have used local Sitka and Engelmann spruce, Port Orford cedar, Lombardy poplar (for a good, light viola), and superbly figured Oregon maple with thin, close annual rings. My favorites are Engelmann spruce and Oregon maple, both old, slow growth, high altitude. Of course, this is a personal view.

GLUE

Use only traditional (clear) hot hide glue on INSTRUMENTS. Hot water is used with it to thin, clean up, release, reflow, and to swell wood joints together.

For work on BOWS, these exceptions are made:

Liquid Hide Glue. Sparingly to hold the wedge in the frog.
Aliphatic Glue. To attach wrapping and grip.
Cyanoacrylates, Specialized (toughened and thickened). To repair ebony and pernambuco.
Cyanoacrylate, Thin. A drop in the end of the hair and on the thread tie instead of rosin.

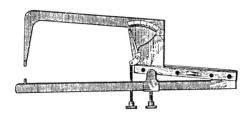

GRADUATION CONTROL

After the maker has selected a type of graduation, he still needs a method of "quality control" to provide consistency and predictability.

The traditional way of graduating is to use depth controlled guide holes, followed by caliper checks, feeling the stiffness and listening to the tap tone(s), and alternately scraping until satisfactory.

In recent years, Chladni pattern testing has been popularized. This adds visual feedback during graduation, and provides precise determination of the tap tone(s). It is clearly presented in *Plate Tuning for the Violin Maker, C.M. Hutchins, VSA Journal, Vol. VII, No. 1*. Another supplementary method, described by K. Leonhardt, uses the translucency of wood as a way to assess the evenness of graduation.

As a former engineer, I have of course tried Chladni testing, and (on another subject) experimented with objective testing of finished violins. I designed and built equipment to put a standard noise (all frequencies) into the violin and record its "signature" output sound. I have lost interest in these technological approaches. The violin has so many variables and nuances, so much that is subjective and artistic. Scientific methods can be applied to gain new insights, but it is finally art that matters in violins.

Oregon Maple

AFTERWORD

(Fiddle Philosophy)

MAKING AND REPAIR

The artistry of the maker and repairer are different, but are not infrequently found in the same person. The maker creates an object of art that he signs and presents as his own. Repair work, however, is usually anonymous, the repairman endeavoring to merge his work inconspicuously, perhaps invisibly, into that of the original maker.

The maker has control of his complete production process and is in a better position to predict the effect of a change. The repairer works on many instruments of many makers. He has to solve many different problems and the same problems in many different contexts. He too has to be uncompromising, not calling the work complete until it is right, but recognizing when it is.

The maker and repairer have this in common, that neither is likely to get rich from his labor, although the maker may receive posthumous credit.

Repair work falls into two major classes, which may overlap. These are

DAMAGE REPAIR: Correction of accidentally or environmentally caused harm to the structure or finish. (Breakage, cracks, scratches, etc.)

ADJUSTMENT: Correction of anything affecting tone or playability, whether an original defect, or caused by age, use, neglect, or inept repair. (Replacement or modification of bridge, post, bar, fingerboard, etc. Restoration of arching, neck angle, bow camber, etc. Renewing expendable parts, pegs, strings, bow hair, etc. Regraduation, etc.)

The repairer must know the construction details and functional principles of whatever he works on. He should be a violin maker, a player, and a critical listener before doing certain adjustment work. And he needs the skill and experience from having worked on many instruments in the tradition of the craft.

Repairs may also be classified according to artistic elegance or mere functional correctness. Only work of the highest artistic level and skill is appropriate on fine instruments, but functionally correct, workmanlike (never crude) repairs may be acceptable on mass produced school instruments. The student especially needs a good sounding, easy playing, and affordable instrument.

SOME RULES OF REPAIR: Avoid removing original wood or varnish whenever possible. On instruments of historical value, do nothing irreversible and record reversible changes. Market value and musical value are not directly related. The repairer seeks to maintain the former and optimize the latter, the dealer vice versa. This is oversimplified; the aims and the men may overlap. Inept repair and erroneous appraisal are both reprehensible. *Knowledge of one's limits is the first rule.*

NEW AND OLD

Stringed instruments are functional objects of art. Beautiful to see and hear, pleasing to possess. The value of a particular violin is based on many subjective and artistic factors and cannot be objectively measured. Esthetic and functional design, maker, material, appearance, workmanship, preservation, history, provenance, associations, and certification by respected experts. Not just tone, playability, and carrying power.

A real part of the maker's life has gone into a fine violin, as well as the efforts of careful restorers and inspired performers, all of whom must have been, at least in the first sense of the word, amateurs (lovers) of the violin.

Aging and the natural selection process undeniably tend to give old violins a lovely sound, but a new violin can sound very well, as well as be a very sound investment. The importance of the violin runs a poor second to that of the performer, in any case, although no one would deny the inspirational value of a classic instrument to the performer. A great performance demands a good, not necessarily an old, instrument, but certainly one in good repair and adjustment.

Classical musicians and violin makers are naturally conservative, but perhaps there is an excessive tendency today, promoted by competitions, to discourage artistic originality whether in performance or in violin making. Good violins need not (and do not) sound or look exactly alike, as long as they are within the established classical context, as long as they look and sound like beautiful violins.
I appreciate fine old instruments for their beauty and for what I have learned from working with them. Nevertheless, I am sure that more and better new violins are being made now than ever before.

ABOUT THE AUTHOR

Born in Indiana in 1936, he studied, worked, and traveled widely, always keeping an interest in the violin. He made his first in 1969 while an engineer in California. He started a violin repair business in 1977, full time since 1983. In 1985 he moved to Oregon where he has a violin shop near Salem. He is experienced in the repair of all instruments and bows of the violin family and occasionally makes violins, violas, and cellos. He would like to thank his wife and children, his violin maker friends and associates, and his customers for their support. Doubtless they are all glad that "the book" is done so he can spend more time in the shop again. And so is he.

Henry A. Strobel
Violin Maker
Oregon 19

"STROBEL Henry A. Luthier américain né in 1936. Il fait son premier violon en 1969 et s'établit en 1977 à Novato (Californie). Petit modèle personnel, grand modèle inspiré de Guarneri et vernis sombre à l'alcool sur fond clair à huile. Etiquette n° 3665."

Dictionnaire Universel des Luthiers, Vol. 3,
Les Amis de la musique, Brussels, 1985

OCTAVE:	1	2	3	4	5	6	7
B	61.74	123.47	246.94	493.88	987.77	1975.53	3591.07
A# (Bb)	58.27	116.54	233.08	466.16	932.33	1864.66	3729.31
A	55.00	110.00	220.00	440.00	880.00	1760.00	3520.00
G# (Ab)	51.91	103.83	207.65	415.31	830.61	1661.22	3322.44
G	49.00	98.00	196.00	392.00	783.99	1567.98	3135.96
F# (Gb)	46.25	92.50	185.00	369.99	739.99	1479.98	2959.96
F	43.65	87.31	174.61	349.23	698.46	1396.91	2793.83
E	41.20	82.41	164.81	329.63	659.26	1318.51	2637.02
D# (Eb)	38.89	77.78	155.56	311.13	622.25	1244.51	2489.02
D	36.71	73.42	146.83	293.67	587.33	1174.66	2349.32
C# (Db)	34.65	69.30	138.59	277.18	554.37	1108.73	2217.46
C	32.70	65.41	130.81	261.63	523.25	1046.50	2093.01

VIBRATIONS/SECOND (HERZ)

This table includes the fundamental range of the violin family. It is in equal temperament, each semitone higher than the preceding by the twelfth root of 2. Compared with the intervals of just intonation, for example, the octave is identically 2/1, the fifth is about 2 cents (2 percent of an equally tempered semitone) smaller than 3/2, the fourth about 2 cents larger than 4/3, the major third about 14 cents larger than 5/4, the minor third about 16 cents smaller than 6/5.

HARMONICS:
Bowing while lightly touching the string at 1/2 its length sounds an octave higher, 1/3 of its length an octave and a fifth, 1/4 of it a double octave, 1/5 of it two octaves and a third, and 1/6 of its length two octaves and a fifth.
For example, in tuning the bass, touching the D2 (2nd) string at 1/3 of its length sounds A3. Then touching the A1 (3rd) string 1/4 of the way also sounds A3. This is repeated to tune the 4th string to the 3rd at E3, and the 1st to the 2nd at D4.

BASIC VIBRATING STRING:
The simplified relationship is that $f = (2L)^{-1}(T/m)^{1/2}$, where f is the frequency of vibration, L is the string length, m is the mass per unit length, and T is the tension. For example, halving L doubles the frequency, whereas doubling both the mass and the tension keeps the frequency the same (but is louder).